COACH
YOURSELF
FIRST

A COACH'S GUIDE TO
SELF-REFLECTION

MARK BISSON

Matador
9 Priory Business Park,
Wistow Road, Kibworth Beauchamp,
Leicestershire. LE8 0RX
Tel: 0116 279 2299
Email: books@troubador.co.uk
Web: www.troubador.co.uk/matador
Twitter: @matadorbooks

ISBN 978 1788037 082

British Library Cataloguing in Publication Data.
A catalogue record for this book is available from the British Library.

Typeset in 11pt Aldine401 BT by Troubador Publishing Ltd, Leicester, UK

Matador is an imprint of Troubador Publishing Ltd

To Jade and Gemma, you are stronger than you think you are. Life events have shaped you and made you resilient and reflective. My wish is that you continue to build your own sense of independence and that you lead happy lives surrounded by those that you love and care for. Also to my sister Jackie, thank you for sharing the pureness of your heart with me. I dedicate this book to you all.

"By three methods we may learn wisdom: first, by reflection, which is noblest; second, by imitation, which is easiest; and third, by experience, which is the bitterest."
Confucius

Contents

Part two – Creative approaches to self-reflection

Part three – The role of supervision in supporting self-reflection

Part four – Your future journey

Foreword

You are in for a treat. There are few, if any, texts written about the science and the art of self-reflection. Mark Bisson has produced an important resource for all who aspire to be a professional coach. This book explains well-researched theories and the practice of self-reflection through the lens of a practitioner who has invested hugely in his own development. The reader is privileged to share his learnings, his reflections and his confidences which have resulted in a tried and tested toolkit for application in many reflective situations.

Whether you are a coach, supervisor or trainer, in-house or freelance, you will find much to support your development. This is a book which helps you learn in a practical way whilst providing a solid foundation of well-researched principles on which to base your new knowledge and experiences, if you are new to coaching or have been doing it for some time. You will find ways to stretch your thinking and creativity, and extend your skills. How far you take it is up to you.

The exercises and reflective routines can be used alone or within peer coaching/supervision groups and could even be taken into your coaching sessions to aid clients in this fast-paced world of task orientation – how often do your clients have the luxury of reflection? Do they even know how to do it? Not only are we living in a highly complex and changing world, with the speed of the resulting stressors come increased mental health instabilities and confusion. The practice of self-reflection gives us a reason to pause, to stop and think about our desires for the standard of our professional work and how to align this with our holistic wellbeing, giving us new-found confidence to support our clients and ourselves in our challenges.

We can choose to continually develop our thinking and understanding or to get left behind in the treacherous swamp of stagnation. Mark's understanding of learning styles makes this as easy as possible for us. If you are an experiential learner, start with the pragmatic Part two and then return to Part one to underpin and consolidate your learning. However, theorists should start with the principles of reflection, covered in Part one, before moving to Part two to test those theories in practice.

Mark generously offers to listen to your stories, your comments and feedback – please take this gift as it is offered. I wish you well with your journey. I know it works because I have seen, experienced and taught it first-hand. Now I invite you to join us in the exciting discoveries of self-reflection.

Dr Sally Vanson

Stiffkey, Norfolk. 2016

Preface

As a new coach beginning to practice at the turn of the millennium I was enthused by the thought of a lifelong learning journey in my chosen profession. I could instantly see the benefit of reflecting on my coaching sessions to support the development of my practice. I took a traditional approach and began to use a reflective log. However, the reality was that what I logged was more of a description of the topics the coachee brought to the session and the models and tools I used. I also noted the actions the coachee had decided to focus on. I am a marker and assessor for the Institute of Leadership and Management (ILM) and I regularly see my initial approach replicated in the coaching portfolios of those undertaking coaching qualifications. My truth was that when I qualified as a coach there was little reference to what best practice was in terms of self-reflection within a focus on developing my coaching practice. Instead, the focus was on learning and trying out models and tools. I developed my approach to self-reflection over many years of reading, researching and academic learning which culminated in an MA in applied coaching.

I found excellent generic books on the topic of self-reflection and specific chapters in coaching books by thought leaders in the profession. However, I could not find any book which specifically focused on guiding coaches and coach supervisors in developing their ability to self-reflect using a variety of creative approaches.

This was the embryonic catalyst for this book. I am known as someone who can turn strategic high-level thinking into practical solutions and I consider myself to be more of a pragmatist than an intellectual. My hope for you as you progress through the book is that you can see a link between the theory relating to reflective learning and the content that aims to provide you with practical guidance, tools and techniques which match a variety of learning styles.

As I began my journey as an author, a publishing company in the United States asked me a question which made me sit back and think about the potential impact of my book on the wider system. The question was "What is your vision for the book and how do you hope it will give back to humanity?"

My considered response was that I wanted to write a book to support coaches and coach supervisors in developing their ability to self-reflect on their practice and gain new insights regarding themselves and their clients. I also recognised that the topic of the book had the potential for attracting a broader audience for leaders and managers looking to reflect on their leadership approaches. My hope is that the book will enable you to learn more reflectively and become better practitioners in the service of your clients and those you work with.

Acknowledgements

I owe an enormous debt of gratitude to those who have supported me on my journey of writing my first book. Firstly my wife Jackie, with whom I have a wonderful shared personal and professional language. Thank you for your support and belief in me.

My enduring thanks also to Dr Sally Vanson who has been such an inspirational influence on my personal transformational journey. You have supported me on my journey of knowing myself and have been a 'caring hand on my shoulder' with invaluable challenge and support. You held a mirror up and encouraged me to break out of my old skin and you challenged me to bring the creative, playful me to my coaching practice and to the new me as an author.

I reached out to a number of colleagues and my LinkedIn network in my search for knowledge from other authors who had been on the tricky journey of being first-time authors. I would particularly like to thank Richard Summerfield, author (Loving Leadership) for his insights and for sharing his learning. I would also like to thank Steve Harding (The Janus Trilogy) for sharing his experience of self-publishing.

A number of friends and colleagues offered to read my draft manuscript and I would particularly like to thank Dr Daniel Marshall for giving so freely of his time and for the valuable input and feedback.

Having an encouraging and supportive family has also been key in keeping me motivated during the inevitable difficult moments. Thank you for listening to me and for keeping any doubts you may have had about me having what it takes to be an author to yourselves!

I also want to thank Justin Sachs for contacting me with a request for a book proposition. Your email lit my fire as an author. You also provided a high-quality online book writing course which I learnt so much from.

Thank you also to my colleagues at Marbral Advisory for your support and particularly to Jo Buchanan for your advice regarding the technical elements of publishing and marketing my book. I also owe a debt of gratitude to Kelley at the Kingston Coaching group who helped reignite my energy when I had become bogged down in the publishing process.

I wrote these acknowledgements in a coffee shop in St Helier on the island of Jersey in the Channel Islands after being fogged in overnight following a business meeting. I want to thank Jersey and the people I know and love on the island for offering me the roots I have longed for all my life. This has provided me with the certainty and stability from which I can be authentically me in the world. I would not be the person I am without you. Thank you for being my sanctuary and the place I love to return to, where I feel centered and at peace.

PART ONE

Theory and research related to self-reflection

Introduction

I believe it is important for readers of this book to understand a summary of the theory and research related to self-reflection as it sets the context for part two which focuses on providing practical guidance on a variety of creative approaches and techniques to support you on your journey of self-reflection. This journey in my experience does not have an end destination. It is a lifelong learning journey which for me is embedded in who I am as a human being. As an illustration I would like to tell you this short story. A few months ago I arranged to have lunch with my daughter Jade who works in London. We met at a café close to her office and ordered our food. As we were waiting for our order to arrive we got into conversation. I said that I had been reflecting on how I had been as a father to her and her younger sister Gemma. I then shared some of my reflections on how I could have been a better dad and what I was trying to change. It was at this point that she stopped me mid-sentence and said, "Stop worrying all the time, I just want you to be a normal dad." I was taken aback and wasn't sure what she meant. So I asked her about her definition of normal. She replied, "Dad, you are always analysing and thinking about stuff. That isn't normal and all I want you to do is to have a gossip with me." After a large intake of breath and reflective silence on my part I went on to explain that I couldn't and didn't want to stop analysing and reflecting. It was part of my make-up, which had been reinforced by my academic journey and my job as a professional coach. I said I enjoyed being me and didn't want to change and nor could I unlearn what I now knew about myself. My reflection after the conversation was that once you start a journey of self-reflection there is no going back and it pervades all aspects of your life. And yes, I am working at improving my gossiping skills with my daughter!

Writing this book has been a learning process in itself and I would like to build an ongoing relationship and dialogue with those who read it. With this in mind I welcome your reflections and would love to hear your stories as you progress on your journey of reflective learning as a coach or coach supervisor. Equally, if you are reading this book to gain knowledge about self-reflection and how you can use it in your life, I am interested to find out what worked for you and what didn't as well as your challenges and dilemmas. I have set up an interactive forum with the intention of creating a self-sustaining community of reflective practitioners. You can sign up on my website so please do make contact with me at risecoachingandmentoring.com.

The next section aims to provide a definition of self-reflection in generic terms and specifically as it relates to the coaching profession. Before you move on, at this point I would encourage you to develop your own self-reflection log template which you can use to reflect as you work on the challenges set at various points throughout the book. You can use the template which I have created or develop your own.

Reflective log template example

Date

Topic/event

What happened?

What did I think at the time and what additional thoughts do I have now?

What may others have thought?

What did I feel at the time and what do I feel now?

What is my one overriding emotion in relation to the topic/event?

What do I believe to be true about this?

How do these beliefs impact my practice?

What have I learned about myself?

How does this challenge the view I have of myself as a coach/supervisor

What would I do differently/more of/less of in the future?

Review of my own reflective processes

Reflective challenge

Develop a self-reflection template either using the one provided as a starting point or develop your own. Think about what you want to learn about yourself and incorporate appropriate reflective questions into your template.

A definition of self-reflection

It is part of the human condition to be introspective and to have a desire to gain a better understanding of ourselves and the rest of humanity. This is one of the key characteristics which sets us apart from other species on the planet. As early as the fifth century BC, the Greek philosopher Socrates advocated for all humans to 'know thyself'. In more modern times, scholars at the time of the Enlightenment proclaimed a revitalised conviction that, in the words of the German philosopher Immanuel Kant,

> *"Man is distinguished above all animals by his self-conscious-ness, by which he is a 'rational animal'" (1999).* Korsgaard used this quote to argue that *"human beings have devel-oped a specific form of self-consciousness, namely the ability to perceive, and therefore to think about, the grounds of our beliefs and actions as grounds" (*2004, p85).

A century later Sigmund Freud argued that human behaviour is, to a large extent, controlled by the unconscious mind. Developing self-awareness of our unconscious mind is often the starting point for deeper self-reflection as a coach. The Oxford Dictionary defines self-reflection as 'serious thought about one's character and actions', whereas the psychology dictionary referring to self-reflection says it is 'the examination and contemplation of our thoughts and actions'.

Freire (1972) argued that the creation of awareness in the conscious mind brings a reflection on material

reality, whereby critical reflection is alr
Freire's concept of praxis emanates from
that action and reflection are indissolubly u
this position, Freire pronounced that "*Refle*
action is sheer verbalism or armchair revolutio
without reflection is pure activism, or action for action's sake"
(Freire 1972, p41). Boud, Keogh and Walker argue that
reflection is "*'meta-thinking' (thinking about the relationship*
between our thought and action in a particular context)" (1985,
p147). This can also be described as temporal comparison
which is defined as the comparison of your current self
to your past self.

Rolfe (2011) argues that reflection is "*a natural human*
activity" (2011, p4). However, this activity often has no
structure to it and could equally be described as cerebral
wandering with no end product. The purpose of this
book is to guide coaches and supervisors in learning
how to self-reflect in a deeper, structured way where the
focus is on learning and creating new awareness which
leads to action.

Self-reflection is a voluntary choice and can be used
as a self-regulatory process. I believe that we all have
the capacity to improve and develop our ability to
self-reflect. Rolfe states that critical reflection is "*a*
difficult and challenging undertaking but that is no reason for
not attempting it" (2011, p9). I would go a step further
and state that self-reflection is a critical element of our
ongoing development as professional coaches and coach
supervisors. Therefore you shouldn't just attempt it,

'ou should instead aspire to mastery in self-reflection as part of a lifelong learning journey. To do otherwise is not being the best you can be for your clients.

The benefits and limitations of self-reflection

I have made the assumption that if you are reading this book you are signed up to the principle that self-reflection is a positive practice to undertake as a professional working in the coaching profession. Nevertheless, I thought it would be useful to dwell for a moment on the benefits and the potential risks and limitations relating to self-reflection.

I view self-reflection as an essential component of my continual learning journey. It has provided me with new insights into myself and has enhanced my understanding of others, both in my professional life and, more holistically, in my relationships with family and friends. Self-reflection has regularly enabled me to expose and challenge my assumptions. It has also facilitated the transfer of knowledge and encouraged me to adapt my map of the world in Neuro-Linguistic Programming (NLP) terms and allowed me to learn from my experiences in the profession over the last sixteen years. Hellison and Templin state that:

"by reflecting on practice, a coach may expose his or her perceptions and beliefs to evaluation, creating a heightened

sense of self-awareness, which in turn may lead to a certain openness to new ideas" (1991, p9). Johns describes a benefit of reflection, stating that *"it opens up a clearing where desirable practice and the barriers that constrain its realisation can be unconcealed and where action can be planned to overcome the barriers whatever their source"* (2013, p7).

In his earlier work, Johns (1995) indicates that reflecting on practice is difficult and advocates the use of detailed models which guide and support coaches. The purpose of this book is to provide a practical guide to support you with models, tools and approaches to satisfy different learning styles. Dewey, who was considered to be a thought leader on reflection in the early twentieth century, described three attributes which he considered were required in order for someone to participate in reflective learning. Open-mindedness, which he described as *"an active desire to listen to more sides than one, to give heed to facts from whatever source they come and to give full attention to alternative possibilities"*. Wholeheartedness, which is being *"absorbed in an interest"* and responsibility to ensure that the improvements in practice are accepted internally through *"securing integrity in one's beliefs"* (1933, p30). This links with dialogic reflection which involves looking at an event from a disassociated perspective and investigating the experience using qualities and judgements. Although Dewey's work was not focused on the coaching profession specifically, I believe that it does provide a framework for what is required to be an effective reflective coach.

Supporting this view, Paterson and Chapman contend that:

> *"The purpose of reflection is to work on what is already known and add new information with the result of drawing out knowledge, new meaning and a higher level of understanding"* (2013, p1).

There are of course limitations to reflective practice. Davies lists the following possible limitations:

- *Not all practitioners may understand the reflective process*
- *May feel uncomfortable challenging and evaluating own practice*
- *Could be time-consuming*
- *May have confusion as to which situations/experiences to reflect upon (2012, p10).*

Other psychological barriers to reflection include fear of judgement or criticism, defensiveness and professional arrogance. I would add to this list a lack of knowledge regarding the theory of self-reflection and reflective practice as well as a lack of knowledge of practical models and techniques to use as a framework. A coach supervisor's ability and breadth of knowledge and experience in reflective practice would also be a limitation for the coach in undertaking self-exploration in a safe, confidential and truly collaborative environment.

Reflective challenge

Reflect on which definition of self-reflection most resonates with you and explore the reasons for that resonance in your reflective log/diary. You may also want to write your own definition and then review it once you have reached the end of the book.

The coaching profession's position regarding self-reflection

Many of the leading associations in the field of coaching list self-reflection within their core list of competencies. The EMCC (European Mentoring and Coaching Council) and Association for Coaching's code of ethics includes the following statements under the heading of ongoing supervision:

- To support their learning and ongoing professional development, members will engage in regular reflective practice.
- Members will reflect regularly on their client work and coaching and mentoring practice and their professional and personal learning and development.

The International Coaching Federation ICF code of ethics also includes expectations of credentialed coaches in respect of searching for continued self-awareness, self-monitoring and self-improvement. However, the Association for Professional Executive Coaching and Supervision (APECS) and the Association for Coach Supervisors make no explicit reference to self-reflection in their codes of ethics, with more generic statements instead focused on members being committed to their own learning and development. The Worldwide Association of Business Coaches (WABC) have a section in their coaching competencies on knowing yourself – self-insight and understanding, having ready access to thoughts and feelings and being aware of how they affect behaviour.

In summary, there isn't a consistent view regarding self-reflection in the codes of ethics of professional coaching associations. I believe this is symptomatic of a profession which is still finding its place in the world and what the expectations of members of those associations should be. An example of this is that the EMCC and the Association for Coaching are endeavouring to unify with the publication of a joint code of ethics. However, other associations such as the ICF still remain unconvinced of the unification argument. The positive stance some associations have taken by including an explicit reference to self-reflection in their codes of ethics and core competencies is backed up by research. McGonagill (McGonagill study O'Broin & Palmer 2009) suggests that the ability to reflect upon oneself and on one's practice is a core competency of coaches. My experience is that there is very limited reference to self-reflection on most coach training courses, with the emphasis being more on self-managed learning in the acquisition of knowledge and skills. However, in contrast, coach supervision qualifications tend to include a significant amount of course content on deep reflection both individually and in group settings. I believe that the inconsistent view across professional associations regarding the importance of self-reflection is not helpful. A consistent view would provide clarity to the coaching profession and enhance credibility for those that use our services.

Reflective challenge

Consider what you would add to your coaching or supervision agreement templates regarding self-reflection.

The research base relating to self-reflection

There is evidence from researchers that self-reflection cannot be learned from books in isolation (Houston & Clift's study as cited in Ertmer & Newby 1996). Hoogeboom (2011) examined the predictive value of three different interventions aimed at enhancing self-reflection and postulated that an experiential learning[1] approach was required to optimise the ability to self-reflect (Kolb's study as cited in Von Wright, 1992). It is suggested that this approach ensures integration with pre-existing knowledge, skills and behaviours. Hoogeboom argues that the integration of both deductive and integrative processes is challenging. However, Hoogeboom considers this to be a critical link between knowledge and control of the learning process

---

1 Experiential learning is learning by doing and then reflecting on the experience in order to identify the learnings taken from the experience.

(Ertmer & Newby 1996; Simon's study and Vermunt's study as cited in Ertmer & Newby 1996).

There is limited academic research with regard to measuring self-reflection. Grant et al. (2002) developed what they called The Self-Reflection and Insight Scale. The scale distinguishes between the motivation to engage in self-reflection and the actual act of self-reflection and incorporates a subscale which measures insight. Within teacher education training, social work, higher education, medicine, nursing and other caring professions, reflection is described as a key tool for professional development (McGlinn 2003; Mueller 2003; McAlpine et al. 1999; Lyon & Brew 2003 as cited in Hoogeboom's study 2011).

Lysaker et al. (2010 as cited by Hoogeboom 2011) argue that impairments in the ability to be self-reflective might lead to a slower learning curve. They indicate that low self-reflection could result in difficulties discriminating goals, plans and emotionally laden intentions which has a negative impact on learning. In addition, without being able to reflect upon your thoughts and feelings, it might be difficult to learn about your behaviour and develop yourself after having received feedback at work. Researchers have also gone as far as to say that the lack of support hinders the development of reflection (Dornan et al's study as cited in Mann et al. 2009 as cited by Hoogeboom 2011).

So, whilst self-reflection is seen as a core competency within the coaching profession for the development of practice, there is limited research that considers the relationship between professional growth as a coach and self-reflection. There is, however, a clear direction of travel in the profession towards reflective practice.

Reflective challenge

Using your reflective log, consider your overarching coaching or supervision philosophy and how you include reference to your own self-reflection in your philosophy.

What is reflective learning?

One definition of reflective learning describes it as "*paying critical attention to the practical values and theories which inform everyday actions, by examining practice reflectively and reflexively. This leads to developmental insight*" (Bolton 2010, p19).

In practice-based professional learning settings, reflective learning can be an important tool to support individuals learning from their own professional experiences as opposed to settings where formal teaching or knowledge transfer have more prominence. The approach is used widely in professional development in the sectors of education, nursing, medicine and social care.

There are a number of alternative definitions of reflective practice. In the last thirty years, Donald Schön has become known globally as a thought leader in the field of reflective practice. He describes the concepts of 'learning in action' and 'learning on action' in his book *The Reflective Practitioner* (Schön 1983). However, John Dewey was writing about reflective practice and the combination of experience, interaction and reflection in his work related to the teaching profession some fifty years earlier (Dewey 1933).

The Chartered Institute of Personnel and Development (CIPD) have produced a statement which describes what reflective learning enables you to gain:

- To accept responsibility for your own personal growth
- To see a clear link between the effort you put into your development activity and the benefits you get out of it
- To help see more value in each learning experience, by knowing why you're doing it and what's in it for you
- To learn how to 'learn' and add new skills over time.

Reflective practice was introduced by Donald Schön in his book *The Reflective Practitioner* in 1983. However, the concepts underlying reflective practice are much older. John Dewey was among the first to write about reflective practice with his exploration of experience, interaction and reflection. Other researchers such as Kurt Lewin, Jean Piaget, William James and Carl Jung (1964) were developing theories of human learning and development. Marcus Aurelius's *Meditations* (Hadot, 1998) has also been described as an example of reflective practice.

Dewey's works inspired writers such as Donald Schön and David Boud to explore the boundaries of reflective practice. Central to the development of reflective theory was an interest in the integration of theory and practice, the cyclic pattern of experience and the conscious application of that learning experience. For the last thirty years, there has been a growth in literature and focus around experiential learning and the development and application of reflective practice.

Dewey's seminal work *How We Think: A restatement of the relation of reflective thinking to the educative process* (1933) became a bible for progressive educators in the USA. It is an exploration of thinking and its relationship to learning specifically focused on the education system. It is Dewey's lead which many researchers such as Boud, Kolb and Schön have followed. Dewey considered that reflection was a pre-occupation or dwelling on things which puzzle or disturb us. He viewed reflection and the learning which came from it as a precursor to action. Therefore, much like the focus of coaching, Dewey saw reflection through the lens of being future-focused. Dewey set out a five-step (state) analysis of what he called effective inquiry of thinking but he seemed to struggle to incorporate the impact of emotion. Subsequently, Boud, Keogh and Walker (1985) reworked Dewey's states to incorporate emotions. They defined reflection as an activity in which people 'recapture their experience, think about it, mull it over and evaluate it' (ibid: 19). They reconstructed Dewey's five aspects into three:

- *Returning to experience* – that is to say, recalling or detailing salient events.
- *Attending to (or connecting with) feelings* – this has two aspects: using helpful feelings and removing or containing obstructive ones.
- *Evaluating experience* – this involves re-examining experience in the light of one's intent and existing knowledge etc. It also involves integrating this new knowledge into one's conceptual framework (ibid: 26-31).

Dewey's five thinking states suggest that reflective learning happens after the event. However, Schön (1983) uses the analogy of being on the dance floor and being on the balcony watching the dance to support the definition of *"reflection in action and reflection on action"*. Schön argues that reflection in action occurs when we are in the midst of an experience such as coaching or supervision. Reflection on action occurs after the experience, like standing on the balcony and observing the dance from a disassociated perspective. Learning in Schön's words by descending *"into the swamp of important problems and non-rigorous inquiry"* (1983, p42) has been a key learning which has supported my journey of reflection in action and becoming consciously aware of what I am experiencing, thinking and feeling in the flow of a coaching or supervision session. The model reinforces and gives meaning to who you are as a coach or supervisor and is reflected in how you practice (Murdoch and Arnold 2013).

So, in summary, Schön argues that you can undertake reflective learning in the moment through your lived experience. Schön goes on to emphasise that there is an instinctive, and in many ways creative aspect to this type of reflection. The model he developed focuses on intuitive and artistic approaches to ambiguous situations and events. Schön describes this as *"artful competence"* (1983, p19). His model is aligned with the concept of experiential learning which is a well-established approach in the tradition of adult learning theory.

Reflective challenge

Using whichever self-reflection approach works for you, answer the following questions:

What are your beliefs about self-reflection?

What patterns or themes have you identified in respect of the topics and issues your clients bring to coaching and supervision?

What patterns or themes of issues have you taken to supervision?

What issues do you not take to supervision?

What are your priority areas for development and what informed your conclusion?

Adult learning theory

Rolfe and Gardner (2006) identified two separate discourses of reflective practice. The second discourse identifies reflection as being about personal growth

(Johns 2004, p44). This focus is ontological in that it is learning about ourselves which is aligned with adult learning theory.

Andragogy as a study of adult learning originated in Europe in the 1950s and was then pioneered as a theory and model of adult learning from the 1970s by Malcolm Knowles, an American practitioner and theorist of adult education who defined andragogy as *"the art and science of helping adults learn"* (1980, p43).

David Kolb's four-stage model (Kolb 1984) of experiential learning is a presentation of the approach. In his book *Experiential Learning*, Kolb describes John Dewey, Kurt Lewin and Jean Piaget as the founders of the approach. The model offers a way to understand people's different learning styles and explains the cycle of experiential learning. Kolb defines learning as *"the process whereby knowledge is created through the transformation of experience"* (Kolb 1984, p38). My preferred learning style is accommodative. So I am 'hands on' and I rely on intuition and prefer to take a practical, experiential approach. Indeed it is this style which has come through strongly during the process of writing this book. My academic journey has been the catalyst for utilising an assimilating style, particularly in the research project for my MA. This was not without its challenges as it wasn't a style that came naturally to me as it required me to undertake my own research and analysis rather than relying on others for information.

Kolb explains that different people naturally prefer a certain single learning style. McLeod (2013) indicates that various factors influence a person's preferred style. These could include social environment, educational experiences or the basic cognitive structure of the individual. Kolb indicates that preference is actually the product of two pairs of variables, or two separate 'choices' that we make, which Kolb presents as lines of axis, each with 'conflicting' modes at either end. One axis is referred to as the Processing Continuum (how we approach a task), and the other axis is called the Perception Continuum (our emotional response, or how we think or feel about it).

A key rationale for reflective practice is that experience alone does not necessarily lead to learning. The inference is that a conscious focus on reflection on experience is essential. Anderson et al. (2004) argue that this form of knowledge development is based on a reflection of what a coach does and is often difficult to explain; however it can be seen in how the coach acts. It involves craft, knowledge, and the coach's experiences, values and prejudices.

The linkage with critical reflection

You now have an understanding of the definition of self-reflection and what reflective learning is and how it relates to the coaching profession. So what about the linkage with critical reflection?

Many researchers and academics use the words critical reflection, reflective thinking, reflective practice and reflexivity interchangeably (Black & Plowright 2010). Harvey et al. (2010) and Hatton & Smith (1994) consider that critical reflection may be at a higher, more complicated level that challenges the learner, while Cranton argues that the word 'critical' in the context of critical reflection relates to the ability to bring about transformation in the individual *"…to involve and lead to some fundamental change in perspective"* (1996, pp79-80). However, Fook (2006) has a belief that critical reflection has not been defined with sufficient clarity and advocates that further research is required to produce a basis of understanding which is common and consistent in academic terms and I would argue perhaps across professional boundaries as well. Nevertheless, critical reflection is recognised as a key component in the learning processes of individuals and is advocated in many professions, particularly in the caring, education and supporting vulnerable related professions (Brookfield 2009; Jarvis 2010; Leijen, Valtna, Leijen & Pedaste 2011). Rolfe et al. describe the timing of when critical reflection begins to take place as *"practitioners take control of their own body of experiential knowledge and lay the foundations for a new individualized approach to evidence-based practice"* (2011, p30). In the specific context of coaching, Macpherson in an article in *Questia* magazine describes critical self-reflection as:

> *"…that form of thinking in which the focus of our attention is inward, on some aspect of ourselves, such as our thoughts, emotions, language or behaviour. In addition, the quality of consciousness is questioning or critical in nature and in-cludes the consideration of alternatives".*

Critical reflection is about learning from your strengths and what has gone well in a coaching or supervision session combined with a willingness to explore the lessons to be learnt when a coaching session has not gone well. Indeed Rolfe (2011) is eager to include in his definition of critical reflection the exploration of "*positive aspects of practice*" (2011, p5). I strongly concur with Rolfe's view that "*reflection that is not translated back into practice is of little use and is ultimately nothing more than an empty intellectual exercise*" (2011, p11). Boyd and Foyles in their definition of reflection reinforce this point by stating that:

> "*The process of creating and clarifying the meaning of experience in terms of self in relation to both self and the world. The outcome of this process is changed conceptual perspectives*" (1983, p101).

However, in my experience some of the changes in coaching practice and self-perception can be subtle and may not be immediately obvious to an observer. This does not diminish the impact of the change from the client's perspective but it is harder to analyse quantitatively or qualitatively.

My experience of working in the space of critical reflection has bridged the gap between my academic learning journey and my professional coaching and supervision practice. It has asked me to think deeply about my past and what has made me the person I am, including negative behaviours, limiting beliefs and traits which I have recognised in myself or that others have brought into my awareness through feedback. In the context of being a professional coach, I would argue that critical reflection involves looking at yourself holistically through the lens of self-improvement. Critically, the foundation of this approach is a desire to learn and grow and a desire to be a better human being and practitioner, while Crawley (2005) utilised the research of Hillier (2002) to develop the concept of reflection with a deeper purpose using the term critical reflection. Crawley defines two main reasons for using critical reflection:

- *We can question our routine, convenient, everyday practices and ask questions about what really does and doesn't work.*

- *We can challenge some of our deeper social and cultural thoughts, feelings and reactions, or what Hillier (2002, p7) calls our 'taken for granted assumptions'.*
  (Crawley 2005, p 166)

Clearly, critical reflection has a number of differing definitions. However, what is consistent is the description of critical reflection as a means to achieve self-improvement through action which, in turn, benefits those you interact with both professionally and personally.

Rolfe refers to Ryle (1963) who suggests that "*'knowing that' precedes and informs 'knowing how'*" (2011, p29). The suggestion is that we need to understand the theory before being able to use it in our practice. Whilst it is important to understand the theory and definitions relating to self-reflection, I have not set out to write an academic study of the topic. If you are interested in learning more I would invite you to use the reference list as a starting point for further reading.

Reflective challenge

What does critical reflection mean to you? Think about a time when you undertook a critical reflection of yourself as a coach or coach supervisor and describe your learnings?

Self-reflection theories and models

Kolb's experiential learning theory

Building on the earlier work of Dewey and Levin, the American educational theorist Kolb believes that *"learning is the process whereby knowledge is created through the transformation of experience"* (1984, p38). Kolb's learning theory defines four distinct learning styles which are sometimes also described as preferences. These styles are cross-referenced to a four-stage learning cycle. The model provides an approach to understanding an individual's learning style while at the same time providing a description of the cycle of experiential learning that applies to all humans.

Kolb's 'cycle of learning' is a fundamental principle of his theory. The cycle starts with concrete experiences which then provide the content for observations and reflections. Meaning is then taken from the observations and reflections which are then developed into what Kolb defines as abstract concepts. These concepts then lead the individual to considering the learnings and translating them into actions. These are then trialed experientially and so the cycle continues. Kolb has stated that the ideal scenario is that all elements of the cycle are touched with the inference that sometimes this does not happen.

Kolb's – a four-stage cycle:

1. Concrete Experience – (CE)
2. Reflective Observation – (RO)
3. Abstract Conceptualisation – (AC)
4. Active Experimentation – (AE)

The second level at which the model works is in the definition of four types of learning styles. Each represents combinations of two of the stages of the cycle:

Kolb's four learning styles:

1. Diverging – (CE/RO)
2. Assimilating – (AC/RO)
3. Converging – (AC/AE)
4. Accommodating – (CE/AE)

Kolb describes a learning style as a combination of the decisions we all make on how to approach tasks and how we respond emotionally to the experience of undertaking the task. So, in deciding how to undertake a task our decision will be whether to observe or take action. Our transformative experience will result in a thinking or feeling response.

Previously I described my preferred learning style as accommodating. I therefore rely on my intuition and prefer to take a practical, experiential approach to a task. How I reflect on the task will usually be from a feeling perspective. Through my academic learning journey I have learnt to value the ability of self-reflection, understanding theory and using the knowledge and insight gained to test out hypotheses using the data gathered. This has been a challenge to my natural desire to act on 'gut' instinct rather than logical analysis. In Kolb's model this is defined as an assimilating learning style.

Kolb's model is designed as a guide to our individual preference in how we like to learn. As I have described from my personal experience, it is possible to move between styles but this doesn't necessarily come easily. One of the challenges for me was wanting to jump in at the deep end when I knew that academic learning required me to focus on reading and research from an observer's perspective.

Kolb's four-stage learning cycle model describes how our experiences are translated through reflection into concepts which lead to the identification of new action and then to experimentation. Kolb describes the process of action research as "*a spiral of action and research consisting of four major moments: plan, act, observe and reflect* " (Zuber-Skerritt 1992, p11).

There are other researchers who have critiqued Kolb's model. Fielding argues that "*Learning styles are flexible structures, not immutable personality traits*" (1994, p403). Within this argument is an inferred question regarding how stable or changeable the learning styles are in the context of self-reflection. There is no clear evidence either way, which is reinforced by Robotham (1999) who argued that whether learning styles remain stable over time was not proven.

Smith (2001, 2010) references other criticisms of the Kolb model, including that it does not pay sufficient attention to the process of reflection (see Boud et al. 1983); the claims made for the four different learning styles are extravagant (Tennant 1997); the model takes very little account of different cultural experiences/conditions; the idea of stages or steps does not sit well with the reality of thinking (Dewey 1933); and the empirical support for the model is weak (Tennant 1997).

I believe that, as coaches and supervisors, whichever is our natural learning style, our work leads us into the space of experiential learning. This can take place both within a session and after the situation has occurred. It requires us as practitioners to reflect on our experience, to gain a general understanding of the concepts encountered during the experience. We then test this out in future sessions. Therefore in my opinion Kolb's model does have relevance in the context of coaching and supervision. However Johns describes himself as being *"wary of cyclical or stage models of reflection"* (2013, p36). His view is that self-reflection is not necessarily a linear step-by-step progression. I agree that reflection is a complex and holistic process where the brain considers all the stages as one. I also believe that structuring and compartmentalising our reflections can bring clarity to what it means to self-reflect, particularly for those practitioners at the beginning of their coaching journey and for those coaches and supervisors who value a structured approach.

Reflective challenge

Using the Kolb learning style questionnaire link, identify which is your natural learning style and write a reflective log of what you like about your natural style. Include in the log your reflections about which style you are most uncomfortable with and explore the reasons for this view.

(http://medialab.st-andrews.ac.uk/documents/design_tips/kolblearningsurvey.pdf)

Gibbs' reflective cycle/model of reflection

In his research on self-reflection, Gibbs (1988) builds on Kolb's work and articulates the use of what he terms *"structured debriefing"* in order to facilitate reflection. Gibbs argues the inferred pedagogical implications of Kolb's cyclical model of reflection by stating that *"It is not enough just to do, and neither is it enough just to think. Nor is it enough simply to do and think. Learning from experience must involve linking the doing and the thinking"* (1988, p9). Gibbs is therefore stating that the insights gained from reflexivity must lead directly to informing future practice.

Gibbs' reflective cycle

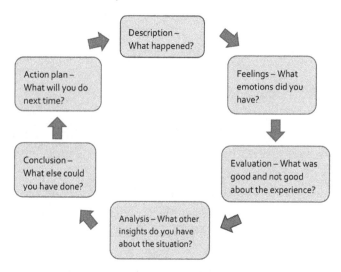

The Gibbs' model of reflection is a cyclical model and therefore has similar benefits and disbenefits as the Kolb model. It encourages the user to think systematically about the phases of an experience. The model encourages the production of a clear description of the event or situation and uses prompt questions to support the user through each phase. The model was developed for an educational context rather than being designed to be used in practical settings.

Johns' model for structured reflection (MSR)

Johns describes reflection as:

> *"being mindful of self, either within or after experience, as if a mirror in which the practitioner can view and focus self within the context of a particular experience, in order to confront, understand and move towards resolving contradiction between one's vision and actual practice"* (2013, p2).

Johns developed his model for structured reflection (2006) through the analysis of dialogue between practitioners and supervisors in the nursing profession. The model also references Carper's (1978) patterns of knowing which are defined as:

- Aesthetics (the art of what we do)

- Personal (self-awareness)

- Ethics (moral knowledge)

- Empirics (scientific knowledge)

To these four patterns, Johns adds a further pattern of reflexivity (How does it connect with previous experiences?). However, as a result of further research, Johns eventually discounted Carper's approach as being too abstract. Instead, he developed what he titled the being available template (BAT) as *"a reflective framework for holistic/person-centred practice"* (2013, pp64-66).

Johns believes the model for structured reflection is one which is particularly useful in the early stages of learning how to reflect. The 'looking in' and 'looking out' is a way some people's natural tendency to judge themselves too harshly can be challenged.

Although there are five clear phases, Johns is quick to point out that the phases and the cue questions within each phase do not have to be undertaken sequentially. They are aimed, however, as Johns puts it, as *"a dynamic movement towards gaining insight"* (2013, p38). Johns evidences that the more frequently the cue questions are used the more they are internalised and become a natural way of working, both in reflection and other aspects of an individual's practice.

Mezirow's transformative learning theory

Mezirow developed his transformative learning theory from the starting position that *"A defining condition of being human is that we have to understand the meaning of our experience"* (1997, p5). The theory considered that transformative learning (Mezirow, 1991a, 1995, 1996; Cranton, 1994, 1996) is a process through which change in a frame of reference can take place. Mezirow believed that we can change our frame of reference through critical reflection. Specifically, he argued that the reflection is on:

> "...*assumptions upon which our interpretations, beliefs and habits of mind or points of view are based. We can become critically reflective of the assumptions we or others make when we learn to solve problems instrumentally or when we are involved in communicative learning*" (1997, p7).

Mezirow used the term subjective reframing to describe self-reflection on our own ideas and beliefs which lead to personal transformations. Mezirow (1994) advocates the consideration of multiple perspectives as opportunities for critical reflection and defines four ways to learn:

- Refine or elaborate existing frames of reference (meaning perspectives)
- Learn new frames of reference (meaning perspectives)
- Transform habits of mind
- Transform points of view

Refining existing frames of reference or learning new ones requires us to engage in deeper perspective transformation when compared, for instance, with changing our point of view.

A consistent pattern of critique of transformational learning is its lack of focus on the importance for social change, social context and cultural context. Clark and Wilson (1991) argue that Mezirow disregards contextual elements (sociocultural and historical) in order to provide a generalised process of perspective transformation and promote individual agency. Mezirow has defended his position by asserting that the impetus for social change comes from the learner and that it may develop out of the transformation process and that cultural context is a crucial element in the transformation process (Mezirow 1991b).

Mezirow argues that *"it is not so much what happens to people but how they interpret and explain what happens to them that determines their actions, their hopes, their contentment and emotional wellbeing, and their performance"* (Mezirow 1991, xiii).

Mezirow goes on to argue that *"transformative learning is learning that transforms problematic frames of reference – sets of fixed assumptions and expectations (habits of mind, meaning perspectives, mindsets) – to make them more inclusive, discriminating, open, reflective and emotionally able to change"* (2003, p58).

My own definition is that transformational learning theory defines how we can make sense of our experiences.

Rolfe's reflective model

Rolfe's reflective model is based on the development model defined by Borton (1970). The model is cyclical and is based on three questions which challenge the practitioner to provide an answer to What? So What? and Now What? The first question encourages a description of the situation/event/dilemma. This then leads into an analysis, evaluation and the taking of learnings using the question So What? The Now What? question prompts the practitioner to consider ways in which they could improve. Rolfe et al. (2001) believed that the third and final stage is of the greatest importance in contributing to practice. Some practitioners may find this model overly simplistic and others may enjoy the clarity and ease of use of this technique which can be embedded in a way of thinking without the need for a detailed understanding of the theory behind the model.

Reflecting in action

Many of the writing techniques discussed in this book are examples of what Schön defined as 'reflecting on action'. Schön (1983) uses the analogy of being on the dance floor and being on the balcony watching the dance to support the definition of *'reflection in action and reflection on action'*. Reflection on action occurs after the experience, such as a coaching or supervision session, which Schön states is like standing on the balcony and observing the dance from a disassociated perspective. The other place to learn from is 'reflecting in action'. Schön argues that reflection in action occurs when we are in the midst of an experience such as coaching or supervision. Schön believes that reflecting in action has far more significance for professional practice and Rolfe adds that this is a *"distinguishing feature of the advanced practitioner"* (2011, p160).

Rolfe argues that reflecting in action includes an ability to turn thought back on an action just taken. So the practitioner is using, in Rolfe's words (which I have revised slightly to remove the gender specific) *"not only conscious of what they are doing but also of how they are doing it"* (2011, p162).

Rolfe identifies that this intelligent action is an *"elusive and difficult concept to grasp"* (2011, p162). Schön sees this as a type of practical on-the-spot experimentation which generates a new understanding and a change in the individual's situation as they reflect in action and *"...becomes a researcher into his own practice, he engages in a continuing process of self-education"* (1983, p299).

In this context Schön defines three forms of experimentation:

- Exploratory experimentation which can lead to discovering something new

- Intended change experimentation which is more deliberate with a focus on an end in mind

- Hypothesis testing experimentation where the practitioner starts with a theory, formulates a hypothesis and then tests the hypothesis 'in action'.

Schön goes on to describe this as a *"continual interweaving of thinking and doing"* (1983, p325) and states his view that all three types of experimentation can be happening at the same time and that an expert practitioner *"does not separate thinking from doing, ratiocinating his way to a decision that he must later convert to action. Because his experimenting is a kind of action, implementation is built into his inquiry"* (Schön 1983, p68).

When I read this for the first time I was quite overwhelmed by the thought that I could aspire to do this in my practice. However, after reading case studies in the healthcare profession, I then recognised that this experimenting can happen with such pace that it was likely that I was performing the experimentation unconsciously. The first stage of reflection in action is an ability to articulate the situation. As coaches and supervisors, we often do this through summarising and paraphrasing and taking the meta-position in the moment. In essence, what I am describing is the ability to be our own internal supervisor. Rolfe describes the process of reflecting on our own reflections as *"meta-reflection"* which he states involves *"doing, thinking about doing, and thinking about thinking about doing"* (2011, p167).

This is amplified by the three levels of thinking in action (Bond and Holland 1998 amended):

Coaching intervention –Intuitive doing

Reflection on the
 intervention doing –Thinking about

Meta-reflection on
the reflection – Thinking about thinking about doing

Learning using Schön's frame of reference *"in the swamp lie the problems of greatest human concern"* (1983, p42) has been a key learning to support my journey of reflection in action and becoming more consciously aware of what I am experiencing, thinking and feeling in the flow of a coaching or supervision session. Schön goes on to state that the practitioner must choose whether they *"stay on the high, hard ground where he can practice rigorously ...Or shall he descend to the swamp where he can engage the most important and challenging problems..."* (1983, p42). In doing so, there is an inference that the compromise is a loss of what Schön terms 'technical rigour'. The model helped me give meaning to the statement 'Who you are is how you coach or supervise' and the importance of being self-aware about who you are in the coaching moment which can lead to improvements in practice.

Murdoch and Arnold, when referencing Schön in relation to coach supervision, state that the low ground is in the *"messy swamps of practice where we come up against grey areas of ethics, morals, values and all aspects of the human condition"* (2013, p97). The key point is that reflective observation is critical to a coach or coach supervisor's ability to facilitate learning and new insight in their clients.

Reflective challenge

Recall a recent coaching or supervision session. Consider at which level of reflection in action you were working at. Write a reflective note on the reasons for your judgement and what role your inner supervisor played at the time.

Reflective writing

Reflective writing provides a vehicle for coaches and supervisors to consider their practice. In the context of self-reflection in the coaching profession, reflective writing can take a number of forms. Shapiro, Kasman and Shafer (2006) consider that reflective writing helps to nurture characteristics in practitioners including narrative competence, emotional equilibrium, self-healing capacity and wellbeing. The practice of writing reflectively is analytical in nature. It requires the practitioner to describe an event, a coaching session, thoughts and feelings together with the meaning and learnings taken. So the focus of reflective writing is not only on description. The reflective practitioner considers meaning, examines what went well and what new insight has been gained and what they might do differently as a result. There is a significant amount of academic research about the benefits of reflective writing. For a slightly quirkier introduction I turned to the Harry Potter novel *The Goblet of Fire* (Rowling 2000, p519). It includes a paragraph regarding the management of excess thoughts. Dumbledore, the chief wizard, is speaking to Harry regarding the volume of his thoughts:

Dumbledore refers to a stone basin which he calls a penseive. The penseive being a receptacle for siphoning out excess thoughts so that they can be considered objectively.

I believe this fictional description of the 'Pensieve' is akin to the process of reflective writing. Like the Pensieve, it provides us with the receptacle to examine our thoughts and spot patterns and links.

Reflective writing provides the opportunity to review experiences objectively at a time when you are not impacted by conditioned or instinctive emotional responses. Over time, as you become more proficient, your reflective writing should include ethical, moral and cultural contexts where these are relevant.

Whatever form of reflective writing you choose, it is important to commit time to reflection. Do experiment and stretch yourself with the different types and styles of reflective writing contained in this book until you find the ones which work best for you.

Reflective challenge

When you experiment with a new reflective writing approach, take some time to analyse the benefits of the approach and its limitations and write down your learnings for future reference.

Exploring ways you might avoid self-reflection

The journey of self-reflection, as I stated earlier, can be a difficult and challenging one. The purpose of this section is to help you explore the reasons why you might avoid it.

Difficult or uncomfortable issues

It could be that a client topic has made you aware of transference[2] and counter-transference[3] which has brought up some strong emotions regarding an issue from your past which you have, up until now, decided not to address.

A topic discussed by a client may have challenged your own beliefs or values. You may have made what you now consider to be inappropriate judgements about a client. You may have recognised that, as part of your internal processing of information, you have made assumptions and do not know whether they are true.

Huber (1995) discusses how fear is masked by a sense of protectiveness and an internal analysis of risks. Huber goes on to encourage an examination of our fear to provide us with an understanding of how our fear process is developed and maintained. In the context of coach supervision Shohet (2008, p203) suggests the following questions relating to fear to reflect on:

2 Transference happens all the time in our daily lives. In the context of coaching it occurs when a client is reminded of someone in the behaviour of others or where previous memories are triggered.
3 Counter-transference occurs where the coach reacts to the transference through their behaviour and emotions.

- *Would you be willing to talk about fear in your sessions either as supervisor or supervisee?*

- *If not, what is holding you back?*

- *What are you finding it difficult to say?*

- *What areas like power, authority, sexuality, race and gender might you be avoiding?*

- *If you hold the possibility that these may sometimes be fear responses, what fear are these interventions hiding?*

- *As a supervisee, do you find yourself wanting to please, editing, unable to say what you want?*

- *Could this be a response to fear and, if so, what is the fear?*

- *What strategies for facing fear have you found useful in the past?*

- *Can they help now?*

Lack of self-awareness

Examples of a lack of self-awareness could relate to your weaknesses or areas for improvement as a coach or supervisor. You could have a lack of awareness regarding how you could be showing bias or discrimination in your practice. You may be failing to acknowledge your fears about something.

The following are steps you can put in place to assist you in using reflection effectively:

- *Preparation – when you enter into a new experience, try to identify opportunities for reflection*
- *Understanding – you need to know what the goals and expectations of critical reflection are*
- *Time to stop and think*
- *A level of objectivity about yourself and the impact of your actions*
- *Honesty*
- *An open, non-defensive attitude to the experience*
- *A focus on the deeper levels of meaning – moral, ethical, social and/or professional issues in addition to your emotional response (Branch & Paranjape 2002).*

Reflective challenge

Use your log to reflect on what thoughts and feelings reading this section has brought up for you? How could you be avoiding self-reflection? What are your next steps in taking this forward to benefit your practice and your own development?

My self-reflection journey – sharing my story

My coaching journey commenced at the turn of the millennium. I was asked to sit on a board accountable for leading the design and implementation of a twelve-week team development programme for 400 teams over a three-year period. I didn't believe I could be an effective board member without understanding what it would be like to be one of the coaches delivering the programme. And so began my passion for coaching and mentoring. Over the next five years, I developed my practice experientially as an internal coach within a large complex organisation with over 20,000 employees. In 2006 I decided I wanted to reinforce my learning through study and took an ILM (Institute of Leadership and Management) diploma in management coaching and mentoring. When I look back now at the assignments I wrote at the time, there is an air of arrogance regarding my level of ability as a coach. It is only with the wisdom of the following decade that I can now see that I was just scratching the surface in terms of my skills, knowledge and indeed my ability to undertake self-reflection. The following decade saw me achieve in a variety of leadership roles in Government. However, I continued to follow my passion for coaching in tandem. I set up an organisational development consultancy which tapped into EU funding for small and medium-sized voluntary sector organisations. I undertook commissions which included facilitating team-building and business strategy workshops as well as one to one and group coaching. I continued to develop my understanding of reflective practice through my academic study. This culminated in an ILM certificate in executive coaching, Neuro-Linguistic Programming (NLP) master practitioner certification and subsequently an MA in applied coaching. I have also trained to be a coach supervisor and have a postgraduate certificate in coach supervision. Through my journey I have learnt that the more you learn the more you become aware of how much more there is to learn. I certainly know that I have improved my ability to self-reflect but sometimes I still feel like a beginner. During my journey I recognised a need to participate in therapy in order to better understand myself and the messages I took from my childhood. Interestingly, ongoing participation in therapy is a pre-requisite for one of the associateships I now have with a leading UK-based coaching organisation. I found the psychodynamic therapy I undertook both extremely challenging and a really positive release and it has certainly provided me with lots of content to work on. It is definitely brave, courageous work. The messages I took from my childhood included the following:

- Be careful, don't take risks as you will hurt yourself
- Playing alone is OK. You can be in your own world but others really aren't interested in being there with you
- Winning and achieving is important as that's when you receive love and recognition but not otherwise
- Competition is fun and exciting and gets the adrenalin pumping as this often leads to recognition
- You need to grow up and be strong and resilient to support yourself as we won't be there for you
- Money is a problem not a joy. You should be careful with money because you don't know what may happen in the future

- It's OK to be focused on yourself to the detriment of your children/others. Think about yourself first because no one else will put you first
- People do things to you which are unjust. It's OK to feel angry about this and harbour resentment about it. It's best to be cynical about people because the reality is you can't trust anyone including your family.

I wanted to be open with you in sharing my messages in the hope that it may prompt you to reflect on the messages you took from your childhood and how they may be impacting your practice and your ability to self-reflect both positively and negatively.

Reflective challenge

Set some time aside to reflect on the messages you received in your childhood, both positive and negative, and consider how they impact your coaching practice. What have you learnt? What next steps do you want to take as a result of the new awareness you now have?

Conclusion

In Part one I have described some of the relevant theories and evidence base which relate to using self-reflection in your coaching practice. It was not my intention for this to be an academic study or to be exhaustive in its nature. I wanted to provide you with sufficient knowledge of the contextual theory in order that you gain an understanding of the theoretical context which sits behind the models, tools and approaches to support your self-reflection which follow in part two.

Part one also provides evidence regarding why self-reflection is critical to being an effective coach or coach supervisor and a summary of the benefits and limitations of self-reflection. I provided my view regarding the inconsistent position which professional associations are currently taking on self-reflection and its inclusion in core competencies and standards.

Definitions of reflective learning have been described and its relationship with adult learning theory and critical reflection. The importance of considering how you might be avoiding self-reflection at a conscious or subconscious level in your practice is emphasised.

I have also shared something about my own personal coaching journey in an endeavour to show some of the challenges that have faced me as I explored my passion for coaching and the role self-reflection has played in enhancing my practice and my journey to be the best I can be in all aspects of my life.

In part two I include my reflections on using the techniques and models over the last sixteen years and some of the reflective challenges I provide have evolved from my experience of using the approaches and techniques. I would welcome your feedback on how they worked with you. You can choose which ones to undertake and you don't have to use them in the order in which they are set out in the book.

Reflective challenge

Now that you have finished reading part one, take some time to reflect on what you have learnt about the theory and research evidence base relating to self-reflection and how you see yourself as a reflective practitioner. You can use the questions set out below or develop some of your own. I would encourage you to reflect intuitively and use the questions which have meaning for you.

What surprised you?

What concerned you?

What would you like to learn more about?

How would you describe your journey of using self-reflection in your practice so far?

How does your journey relate to the theories covered in part one?

How would you describe yourself as a reflective coach or supervisor?

What is your greatest fear with regard to being a reflective practitioner?

What are you particularly looking forward to in reading part two?

What models and tools are you familiar with and how have you used them?

PART TWO

Creative approaches to self-reflection

"Bimadisiwin is a conscious decision to become. It is time to think about what you want to be. The dance cannot be danced until you envision the dance, rehearse its movements and understand your part. It is demanding for every step needs an effort in becoming one with the vision. It takes discipline, hard work and time. Decide to be an active participant in your life journey. It is rewarding. Embrace the joy your vision brings you, it is yours to hold forever. It is freeing, for it frees the spirit. It releases you to become as you believe you must"
(Jones and Jones 1996, p47).

Introduction

The second part of this book looks at a spectrum of approaches, models and tools which you can use to support your self-reflection. Not all of them will be right for you and that is OK. I would suggest that you do push your boundaries and experiment with approaches which may feel uncomfortable to you. Having a healthy level of scepticism will ensure you take a balanced perspective. My learning is that some of the approaches I have been most uncomfortable with have also provided some of my most transformational learning.

The approach I have taken is to group what I consider to be those tools and models which are similar in nature. This is open to interpretation and you may disagree with me and that is also OK. Where I think they provided further richness I have added templates, photographs and links to websites for further reading. I have also referenced my own experiences of using some of the approaches. Please do be mindful that what works for me will not necessarily work for you and vice versa.

The art of effective self-reflection in my opinion has at its core a willingness to be open internally. This openness creates a space for messages to come forward. This could be words, an image or a feeling/emotion. Rickard describes our internal supervisor as *"the combined voice of the best teacher and supervisor we ever had"* (2011, p26).

The following tools, models and techniques are a menu of options for you to use and evaluate. My challenge to you is to try them and reflect on your thoughts and feelings about what works best for you and what doesn't and why.

Reflective challenge

Keep a reflective log as you work your way through the various options and record your thoughts, feelings and learnings from each approach. What worked for you and what didn't and your reflections on why the approach did or didn't work.

Reflective logs

A reflective log is used to record reflections at or near the time of the relevant coaching or supervision session. The log can be structured under pre-determined headings which form the framework for the log. For instance:

- What happened and why?
- My reaction (thoughts, feelings, behaviours)
- What did I learn/discover?
- What am I going to do about it?

The Association for Coaching have developed a reflective record template which is available on their website www.associationforcoaching.com. I have amended the template slightly to accommodate my own learning style preferences.

Client Name		Session Number		Date
• What topics did we cover? • How well did we interact? • What were the main interventions and approaches I used (models, techniques, tools and styles of questioning)? • How well did I keep the client focused on their outcome? • What went well and why? • What worked less well and why? • What would I do differently in a similar situation? • Is there anything else to note down for learning or further exploration with my supervisor? • What view do I have regarding my self-reflective process				

I developed a reflexivity log template which I have reproduced below. It is based on the research I undertook during my academic study for a postgraduate diploma in coach supervision. The log combines feedback from the coach I am supervising and my own reflections after each session. I found that capturing my 'reflecting in action' moments were important to embed my learning and helped me recognise that my ability to do so was improving over time. With my reflections on the supervision relationship I added a narrative to explain my score. The logs supported me in a desire to track changes and patterns in my practice and how I view myself as a supervisor. The template could equally be used as a reflective log for coaching with some revisions.

Coaching supervision session reflexivity template

Name of coach   Date

Supervisee's reflections on last session

Hawkins and Shohet (2012, p239 revised to use the word YOU instead of WE)

1. What have you learnt that you didn't know before you came into the last supervision session and couldn't have arrived at alone?

2. What new capability have you generated in this session?

3. What new resolve have you acquired?

Hawkins (Bachkirova, Cox and Clutterbuck 2014, p394) state that coach supervision has three elements:

- Coaching the coach on their coaching – Resourcing
- Mentoring the coach on their development in the profession – Developmental
- Providing an external perspective to ensure quality of practice – Qualitative

What evidence do you have that I coached you on your coaching practice?

How did I mentor you on your development in the coaching profession?

What evidence do you have of my external perspective supporting you in ensuring the quality of your practice?

Reflexivity

What impact/ influence did I have as coach supervisor during the session?

Building rapport by putting some of myself as interviewer into the session, possibly by raising similar or different experiences (Arksey and Knight 1999).

Did I do this in the session and, if so, what was the impact from my perspective as coach supervisor?

Where did I improvise and what was the impact?

Were there any other reflections in terms of how I conducted the session?

What did I pick up in terms of the supervisee's body language or from their voice?

What is the one thing from the session which challenged me or disturbed me?

What is the one emotion which this supervisee creates in me?

Focusing on bringing 'reflection in action' (Schön 1983) into my consciousness, what new meaning or learning did I take from my inner self during the coaching session?

Commitment to action (Atkins and Murphy 1994)

How will I apply these learnings to my coaching or coach supervision practice?

Notes to take during interview Easterby-Smith (2002, p123)

1. What was the relationship like between coach supervisor and supervisee?

Closed									Open
1	2	3	4	5	6	7	8	9	10

2. What was the attitude of the supervisee?

Disengaged									Engaged
1		2	3	4	5	6	7	8	9	10

3. What is my level of confidence as coach supervisor?

Unconfident									Very confident
1		2	3	4	5	6	7	8	9	10

Taking reflective notes during coaching or supervision sessions – A personal view

Hay gives a balanced view regarding reflective note-taking during supervision sessions. She indicates that some coaches prefer to take notes while others do not. However, she goes on to argue that *"taking notes will give you a better basis than relying on memory, it will indicate to the client that you are paying careful attention and the notes can then be shown to the client as a check on accuracy"* (2007, p23).

From an ethical and core competency perspective I am strongly against taking reflective notes during coaching or supervision sessions. First and foremost, the negative impact on your presence during the session will be significant. Secondly your ability to pick up eye cues and changes in the client's physiology will be impaired if your focus is on writing notes, particularly accurate ones!

I do scribble the odd word or two in sessions. However, the purpose is, for example, to note a metaphor or language pattern which the client has used for possible exploration during the session. I also take note of hand and arm movements by sketching them in order to log the movement and play it into my questions if I think the coachee could take their meaning from it.

I have learnt that if I create the space immediately after a session this enables me to reflect effectively. Trusting yourself that you will recall the key moments during the session is the starting point. As an alternative, some coaches and supervisors I know do record sessions, either using an audio recorder or videos, with the permission of the client of course. They then use the recording for self-reflection or to take to supervision. This can be a helpful way of picking up nuances in terms of body language and language patterns as well as transformational moments. I have used this technique and was surprised at the number of instances where I did not pick up something in the moment which was easy to spot when reflecting on action from the balcony. If you choose to experiment with this approach my advice is not to beat yourself up about what you have missed. Recognise that, as coaches and supervisors, we are making judgements in the moment which we believe are the best ones we can make in service of our client. There are always alternative paths to take and it is important to accept this as part of our journey to being an effective practitioner. That of course doesn't mean feedback from recordings can't provide valuable learning.

Reflective challenge

Make a recording of a coaching or supervision session and then write the story of the session using one of the approaches to storytelling contained in this book.

What have you learnt from this exercise that your usual self-reflection technique would not have picked up?

What are the limitations of using recordings for self-reflection?

Reflective Journals

People keep reflective journals for lots of different reasons. Sometimes it relates to a hobby or supports them in preparing to write a blog. For others it relates to a training regime or a diet. A reflective journal is in essence an ongoing conversation with yourself. It may contain personal stories and descriptions of practice-related events. It involves the recording of deliberate thoughts and an analysis of coaching practice issues and critical incidents. The journal can serve a dual role – to daily reflect on coaching experience and to examine how personal objectives are being implemented and met (Gray 2007). Rosinski advocates the writing of a journal for the practising coach: *"A coaching journal is a valuable tool to help you reflect on your own personal journey, to aid your thinking about what is truly important to you. It is a place where you can capture insights and learn from experience"* (2003, p16). The terms reflective journal and reflective diary are often used interchangeably. The journal should contain the coach's practical knowledge and wisdom, and the coach should re-read entries regularly to determine patterns (Ghaye & Ghaye 1998).

One method of writing a journal within a structure is to use the focused conversation method which is sometimes referred to using the acronym ORID (Objective, Reflective, Interpretive, Decisional). The steps in the method are:

Objective data – Describe a situation from your coaching or supervision practice.

What did you see – including physiology and eye cues, hear, taste, smell, touch? What did you sense?

Reflective data – Describe your reaction. What did you think and feel? What were your kinesthetic reactions?

Interpretive data – describe your interpretation of the data you have gathered.

Decisional data – Make a plan regarding what you will do differently (or the same) the next time you are in a similar situation. What do you need to learn to do differently to manage the situation more effectively?

The following is another example of a reflective journal which I have amended to align with coaching and supervision practice. It is important that the layout and structure of a journal reflects your learning style and what you want to have as your focus. So my advice is not to follow pre-designed templates slavishly but to develop your own using examples as a starting point.

Template for reflective journals

Summary of what Happened (don't describe everything, be selective), What were the critical moments?

-
-
-

Personal reaction

How did I feel about what happened (Did it affect me emotionally and if so how?)

What are my thoughts about what happened?

What did I like or enjoy and why?

What did I dislike and why?

What did I find easy to do or understand and why?

What did I find difficult or challenging to do or understand and why?

What did I fear most about what happened?

New Learning

What did I learn that was new to me?

What insights did this new learning give me?

What new understanding did I gain about myself?

How do I think this might be useful (in my practice, in my studies, in my life)?

What do I need to change, do differently, do more of or do less of in my future practice?

Action to be taken

Is there any action that I will take as a result of what happened and my reflections?

Do I need to acquire any new knowledge?

Do I need to investigate or research further?

Do I need to modify my behaviour?

Another structure for reflective journal writing specifically aimed at coaches has been developed by Francis (1995). The process involves four stages:

- Describing – what did I do? (without judgement)
- Informing – what does this mean? (patterns or principles underpinning the described practice)
- Confronting – how did I come to be this way? (examining social and cultural aspects)
- Reconstructing – how could I do this differently? (alternative views and goals for future critical reflection).

(1995, p232 Stages in personal and professional empowerment amended by M Bisson)

No one method of reflective journaling is more appropriate than another. It is really down to personal choice and what works for you. Holm and Stephenson (1994) developed a set of questions in order to provide a structure to reflective writing. They were written with the medical profession in mind so I have amended the wording to suit the coaching profession. The first step in using this structure is to choose a specific situation and then ask yourself the following questions:

What was my role in this situation? Did I feel comfortable or uncomfortable? Why?
What actions did I take? How did I and my client act? Was it appropriate?
How could I have improved the situation for myself and my client?

What can I change in the future?

Do I feel as if I have learnt anything new about myself?

Did I expect anything different to happen? What and why?

Has it changed my way of thinking in any way?

What knowledge from theory and research can I apply to this situation?

What broader issues, for example ethical, political or social arise from this situation?

What do I think and feel about these broader issues?

Adapted from Holm and Stephenson (1994)

Over time you can use your journal to reflect on your journey as a coach or supervisor by revisiting what you have written. Plummer says the reviewing process is the:

"truly creative part of the work". He adds that *"it entails brooding and reflecting upon mounds of data for long periods of time until it 'makes sense' and 'feels right', and key ideas and themes flow from it. It is also the hardest process to describe; the standard technique is to read and make notes, leave and ponder, re-read without notes, make new notes, match notes up, ponder, re-read and so on"* (2001, p152).

Smith has developed a set of questions to support this process:

- *Are there experiences, situations or understandings that stand out for us? What is it about them that is catching our attention?*
- *Does what we have written in our journals still 'ring true'?*

Have we been fully honest and do the interpretations we made at the time still stand up.
- *From our present standpoint and understanding are there things to question in our writing?*
- *What is missing? Has there been evasion?*
- *Does what we are writing in our journals relate to what we know of other practitioners? Can we see any connection with any broader theories we have been exploring? (1999, 2006, 2013)*

It is important to ensure that the form of writing in your journal is of a reflective nature. This is different to descriptive writing which merely provides a description of the event, topic, problem or dilemma. Whilst dialogic reflection involves reflecting on the event or, from a disassociated observer's perspective, exploring the experience, using qualities and judgements. Bain et al. (1999) argue that coaches can be encouraged to engage in the reflective journal process through questioning as this is a fundamental cornerstone of their practice. Bain et al. also suggest that this can be achieved through working at three different levels of reflection they term as practical, technical and critical. These cover the cognitive aspects including knowledge and process, examination of the themes from the individual's experiences and their values and the cultural context of their practice.

Klug describes a reflective journal as "*a place to record daily happenings*". He goes on to articulate the power of journaling by stating that "*A journal is also a tool for self-discovery, an aid to concentration, a mirror for the soul, a place to generate and capture ideas, a safety valve for the emotions, a training ground for the writer, and a good friend and confidant"* (2002, p1).

I have a small journal notebook which I keep with me in my jacket pocket so it is easily accessible. As well as planning specific time for self-reflection I have been surprised at when and where impromptu reflective moments happen and it is important to me that I have the ability to record thoughts and feelings when they occur. Some coaches I know journal every day and others like me are not journaling slavishly to a time plan but working more intuitively. There are no right or wrong approaches. The right approaches are those which work for you.

Reflective blogs

Reflecting about your coaching or supervision practice using a blog can be an effective method of articulating your thoughts, feelings and learnings and sharing it with others at the same time. Obviously client confidentiality is key, so writing in generalities and identifying patterns and themes is the approach I use. Of equal importance is only going as far as you feel comfortable in sharing information about yourself. A blog can be used for a variety of purposes including posting ideas and sharing your learning from research you may be undertaking. Others can then offer comments and their own reflections which can provide challenge and support.

There are a number of websites which you can use to set up a blog. One example is www.blogger.com which takes you through the steps to set up your blog site. Recent advances in blogging technologies have made the publication of blogs much simpler. Blogs are designed to be read and are referenced by other bloggers. Some experts believe that a blog needs a mission statement that shows the intent of the blog and helps establish your audience. You can also help an audience find you by thinking about who you want to attract and what they care about so that you provide the content which will engage them and keep them returning. I have my own blog on my website www.risecoachingandmentoring. com where I publish about once a month. Other bloggers I know publish far more regularly. I use my blog to share insights I have gained about my own practice, learnings from books I have read and practical tips and techniques I am learning to use in my practice. I also publish articles and updates on my LinkedIn page which is another form of blog.

Blogging can have other benefits including engendering a sense of community with other coaches and supervisors. Sometimes running your own business as a sole trader can feel isolating. Blogging is a way of reaching out to like-minded colleagues and associates. I have included two examples from my own blog to show how it can be used as an effective reflection tool as well as building your credibility as a coach or supervisor.

4th March 2016

Are you looking after your wellbeing?

Recently I have been researching positive psychology as I am increasingly seeing with my coaching clients a pattern of them not looking after their own wellbeing. One of the most eminent authors and researchers in this field is Dr Martin Seligman.

In his book *Flourish*, Seligman argues that positive psychology is about wellbeing and describes five elements:

Positive emotion

Engagement

Accomplishment

Positive relationships

Meaning

He also speaks of a focus on a higher purpose. For instance, my higher purpose when coaching is to support people in their growth and development. I enjoy seeing people achieve their goals and it fulfils my need to achieve through them. So if they are achieving then so am I.

How often do we reflect on what our higher purpose could be? The evidence I have from my sixteen years of coaching practice is that a significant percentage of my clients focus on what is going wrong daily for them, rather than what is going well, and this can have a negative impact on their motivation, their outlook on life and ultimately their wellbeing. To counter this, Seligman suggests an exercise titled "What went well". The exercise works like this. Each night for a week, just before you go to sleep, write down three things that went well that day and then write why you think they went well. This might seem difficult to begin with. My experience is that it does become easier. Seligman says that over time it can become addictive. If you decide to give it a try I would love to hear your reflections after the week is up.

4th November 2015

Avoiding Symbiosis in supervision relationships.

I am currently reading a book titled *Reflective Practice and Supervision for Coaches* by Julie Hay. It includes some great exercises to support supervisors in their self-reflection. Using a Transactional Analysis ego state approach, one exercise encourages the reader to consider how they spend time with their supervisor using the Parent, Adult and Child states. It helped me reflect on how I was in the relationship, what changes I wanted to make and the strengths of the relationship. For instance

I recognised that from the child ego state I am excited to try out the techniques and models my supervisor suggests and this interest in playing comes from my child ego state. However, there are some risks related to the feeling of excitement that I could try out new models and techniques because of my curiosity which may not be in service of the person I am supervising or coaching. I believe taking the time to reflect on any professional supervision relationship is critical in improving how you work together and gaining new insight about yourself.

Storytelling

There is significant evidence that storytelling and the metaphors created within stories can support the stimulation of change in individuals. For some coaches and supervisors, self-disclosure through storytelling is a technique which encourages openness in cultures that close down emotions and any perceived form of weakness. The use of our own metaphors and those used by our clients can enable us to draw out unconscious judgements, bias and assumptions we can hold about ourselves, others and the organisations in which we work. Some of the founding research undertaken on narratives was conducted by Labov (1972). He evidenced that stories were often told for the purpose of communicating about important dilemmas and problem situations. In telling the story, Labov argued the storyteller's perspective on the dilemma or problem and how the storyteller viewed the resolution as it becomes clearer. Indeed in telling the story, the teller communicates what it was like to be actually within the story as actual experience. These stories can then be reanalysed to gain understanding.

The following are guidelines for storytelling based on those produced by Fornreris and Campbell to support medical students in the development of critical reflection skills. I have adapted them to suit the coaching profession:

1. Recall an experience in your coaching or supervision practice that resulted in a feeling of accomplishment, satisfaction, and/or resulted in feelings of discouragement or frustration.
2. Write about this experience in the form of a story with a beginning, middle and end. To help you provide the context for the story, think about the questions Who? When? and Where? as you write the story.
3. Critically reflect on your story and, in so doing, discuss why you picked this story? What are the learnings you have taken from your story and articulate how you think this story will impact your coaching or supervision practice?

McAdams (2008) states that stories give us a deeper insight into lived experience – past, present and our imagined futures. Storytelling is central to defining what it means to be human and through stories we articulate our lived experience in the world and how we make sense of those experiences. Kirkpatrick et al. define storytelling as "*...the individual account of an event to create a memorable picture in the mind of the listener*" (1997, p38). In the context of a coach or supervisor undertaking self-reflection, the storyteller and the listener are one and the same. Storytelling also creates the space for us to reflect on our morals, values and beliefs which can lead to a reframing of our self-identity as a professional coach or supervisor.

McDrury and Alterio (2003, p47) have defined the stages of learning with storytelling:

Stage 1 Story Finding
Stage 2 Story Telling
Stage 3 Story Expanding
Stage 4 Story Processing
Stage 5 Story Reconstructing

Stage 1 is about noticing which story you want to focus on and then Stage 2, story telling, enables you to make sense of the story. Stage 3, story expanding, is the stage where meaning is taken from the story and Stage 4 is where the self-reflective practitioner works with that meaning towards taking learning. Finally, stage 5, story reconstructing is where the transformative learning emerges with a focus on action to be taken.

I believe storytelling is a creative method which can support self-reflection on difficult and sensitive topics. It requires a level of self-awareness and self-honesty in order to tell a story which is your truth. My experience is that it can definitely be challenging, brave, transformative and affirming.

Reflective challenge

Think about a story you want to tell which would support your journey of learning how to self-reflect on your practice. Use one of the storytelling approaches to write your story and reflect on it.

Nine words self-reflection process

Chapman-Clarke (2015) researched approaches to support advanced coaches to become what she termed 'conscious change agents'. The exercise she developed as a result of the research integrates mindfulness with reflective writing. The start of the exercise involves coaching a client through a short mindfulness exercise. However, I have used the nine words approach I am about to describe without the mindfulness element. The approach starts with identification of a dilemma or problem. Once you have identified the topic you then write for three minutes on the topic. You then circle three words from what you have written. You then repeat the process two more times. Chapman-Clarke has laid down some guidelines for 'writing free' which include not crossing anything out you have written, keeping your hand moving and ignoring spelling, punctuation and grammar. You end up with nine minutes' worth of writing and nine circled words. You then explore the nine words using what Chapman-Clarke terms 'mindful inquiry'. Some questions you could use to support your self-reflection are:

- What have I observed about the words?
- What has surprised you?
- What realisation have you had?
- What are you aware of?
- What feelings have been generated in you?

I have used this approach myself and with coaching clients. The form of writing engages me creatively and links with my interest in writing reflective poetry. I have been surprised at the topics and dilemmas I have chosen to write about and how easy it is to write for three minutes in the 'flow'. I have used it to consider my own wellbeing as a coach and thorny ethical dilemmas.

Dialogical writing

Writing dialogically is a style where the writer makes a conscious decision to have an internal conversation with themselves. The nature of the conversation can involve positing ideas and concepts and countering them using a series of questions. The questions are not pre-determined but instead are formed organically as the writing takes place. This enables the writer to explore a situation, pattern or theme in a more unstructured way.

Rolfe refers to this as enabling the writer to *"go wherever the mind goes in response to what has already been written"* (2011, p87). Once issues are identified, the writer provides an internal challenge to themselves with questions like, *"Why did I do that?" "What assumptions did I make?"* and *"What else could I have done?"* (2011, p87). This is followed by an internal dialogue regarding the lessons learnt and knowledge gained. This model of writing provides the opportunity for the coach to go with their intuition and supports the development of an ability towards healthy internal dialogue which leads to what Rolfe terms as an understanding of *"what their writing is saying to them"* (2011, p87). This enables the writer to consider the quality of the judgements they have made and open up possible alternatives, new perspectives and hypotheses.

One way of developing reflection using dialogical writing is to imagine that you are observing a debate among a small group of people who have very different viewpoints on an important subject, situation, dilemma or question. Those who start the debate clearly oppose each other, and their positions seem to be at opposite ends of the spectrum. Other people offer some kind of compromise or look at the issue from a higher or entirely new point of view. You also might imagine two people arguing a case in a debating society or in court. Each argues his or her own position, then the judge or chairperson offers a final opinion that is a compromise or different point of view.

Reflective challenge

Think about a topic, question, situation or dilemma in which you would find it interesting to use a dialogical writing style. Spend thirty minutes thinking and writing using the dialogical writing approach. When the time is up, reflect on your learnings from using this style of writing.

Case Studies

Case study research can be an effective method of bringing greater understanding of a complex issue and can extend experience or add strength to what is already known through previous research. Case studies can bring amplification and clarity via analysis of a limited number of events or conditions and their relationships. Academic and commercial researchers have used the case study research method for many years across a variety of disciplines.

The purpose of case studies in coaching self-reflection is to capture learnings from a specific coaching or supervision session or following the identification of patterns or a dilemma which requires consideration of behaviours, reactions, and patterns in order to reach a conclusion on how to modify your practice. It is a structured process which is often used in academic writing. You might write your reflections in the form of a case study if you are considering sharing your learnings, giving a lecture or if you are reviewing your practice as part of a study assignment for a coaching or supervision qualification. Case studies differ in length; they are usually comprised of about 500-800 words but can go up to over 2,000 words.

Case study template

Title:

1. Abstract

A statement of your question that is the topic or subject of your case study, a statement on how you went about finding the possible answer and a statement on what you found out.

2. Introduction

The aims, context and things you think are linked to the question. Remember to reference any work you are quoting from other sources.

3. Methodology

Or 'How I went about answering the question'.

4. Findings

What were the results of your investigation and what

answers did they give you? You could insert images, sounds or video clips that support your observations.

5. Conclusions

What were the results of your investigation and what answers did they give you? You should refer back to the original question that you have stated in the Introduction. How do the results inform the question? If they don't give the full answer what will you have to investigate further?

6. References

You may have some references that you talked about in the main case study. It could be a research paper, an article or a web page. This is the section where you carefully say where the reader can find that information.

A case study can be exploratory with a focus on creating new knowledge or to solve a problem. It can also be used to test a hypothesis. There is, however, a risk that the coach or supervisor begins to see themselves as a researcher and views the case study from a disassociated stance, having articulated the research topic and then subsequently visioning forward to the expected results and then conducting self-manipulation either consciously or subconsciously to confirm the expected results. This is known as the self-fulfilling prophecy or Pygmalion effect. Popper (2002), suggests in the realm of modern post-positivist scientific thought that the researcher takes the role of disinterested observer. Clearly, as coaches, using the case study approach in order to achieve transformational results requires us to be fully present and personally engaged in the content of what our inner self brings to our conscious minds.

Reflective challenge

Set some time aside to consider what topic you would want to write a case study about. Once you have decided on a topic, think about the environment which would work best to write your case study using the structure provided and how much time you would need. Then go ahead and write your case study. Once you have completed it, consider whether you want to share it and, if so, how you would go about doing so.

Reflective Poetry

During a supervision session I was challenged by my supervisor to engage the creative, playful me in my reflective practice. She suggested that I think about a topic I wanted to bring to supervision and then begin to read poetry using an unstructured and random approach and to look for the meaning I took from the poem which related to my supervision topic. This approach didn't work for me although it may for other coaches. I found myself trying to find meaning which wasn't there and getting frustrated by the process. It did, however, lead me to a transformational place regarding my own self-reflective practice. I decided that I would attempt writing my own poetry immediately after coaching sessions for a period instead of my usual log. I found writing poetry enabled me to connect with my unconscious mind in a flowing, gentle way which I had been unable to do using other writing approaches. I wrote with a stream of consciousness and made little attempt to perfect the words and form of the poem. This flow created new insights about myself and my practice which was confrontational but somehow non-judgemental at the same time. Johns, in a discussion of the benefits of reflective prose poetry, describes it as transforming *"ideas into art – with the intent of revealing meaning"* (2013, p270). I believe that we all have it within us to write reflective prose and that the limitations we have are self-imposed. Writing poetry engages the right side of our brain and frees us up to a deeper creative level of interpretation of our practice. Johns frames it as *"like taking a short cut to the unconscious bypassing the cognitive realm"* (2013, p270).

Johns describes the process of developing a poem based on a story of a real-life situation which he states:

"…helps the practitioner to draw insights which can then be planned within the text as turning points. Language techniques such as litany, repeating phrases, imagery, analogy, signs and metaphors are utilised to hold and communicate meaning" (2013, p270).

If you are interested in this method of self-reflection you could consider attending a poetry workshop to support you in developing your skills. I have reproduced some examples of my reflective poetry on the following pages which illustrate my personal journey. There may be some meaning in my poems for you and, if so, take time to reflect on that meaning as it may not be the same meaning that I took. We are all on our own personal journey of self-reflection after all.

"Scripts"

In my coaching practice
I walk towards a client session
Scripts hidden in my bag

No general practitioner me
My bag is full of wondrous gifts
Which no mere pill can provide

Tools, techniques and models
Reside in my magic bag
I have bestowed this wisdom on myself
Through my learning journey of academic and
experiential kinds

And yet my unconscious mind shouts
You can't possibly have all this in "the muscle"
You need support or you will fail

My inner voice says anyone can read from scripts
you fraud

My preferred learning style persists
And I learn in action as an activist
And so my fellow coaches
Like you I seek the holy grail of mastery
To flow in the moment intuitively

Until I get there I reflect that what holds the greatest power is
Renouncing my anxiety
And wondering am I good enough?

Instead I will be joyous in the knowledge of my growth
And acknowledge the role my scripts have played
In my journey as a coach

"My fear, your blind spot?"

You told me something
Shivers down my spine I named
Why can I see it and you can't?
Is this my stuff or yours?
Am I catastrophising?
With my de bono black hat firmly on

The information you shared
Lights concerns of unprofessional practice
Responded to by my inner voice
Where was the contracting?
How was personal liability considered?

What are the risks to the coachee?
An honest conversation required
Potential parallel process identified
My role as supervisor?
To name what I am sensing
And possible transference

My greatest fear
Your emotional wellbeing
And that of your client
I sensed it, I named it

My confidence growing as a supervisor
Raised insight and awareness
You engage in reflective learning
You articulate your change in practice required
And together we recognise the power of
supervision

"Warmth"

Today I feel the warmth of my coaching journey's
embrace
I sit and reflect on a coaching session
Where I noticed a change in physiology and
energy
Where I know I made a difference
Where the smile from my coachee was enough

As I drive home

I feel the warmth of the sun on my face
And know that this is my place in the universe
I have finally found my seat
Watching my own performance

Hearing the gentle waves of learning and growth
Gently lap onto my cerebral and kinesthetic beach
I whisper to myself, thank you for this gift
And for being my metaphorical cheerleader
Today I feel the warmth of my coaching journey's embrace

"Desperately seeking"

As coaching clients go
You are on the more reflective end of the spectrum
Sometimes you can't find the right words
Expressing yourself is a challenge
Self-criticism and frustration
Fills the space between us

We both desperately want this to work
You seek alternative ways of thinking
I sense you want to be saved
You tell your story
I feel transference
And my stuff surfacing
Struggling to make sense of it

As I grapple with reflecting in action
As prescribed by Schön

Peeling back the layers of the metaphorical onion
Tough stuff for us both
It's time to remove the pressure
To succeed and be perfect

"Forcing blossom"

Coaches and supervisors provide
Water, sunlight and food
For the blossom within our clients to flourish
and grow

Our role as coaches
Connecting neurons in the brain
Combining the power to dream
And a focus on the task-positive network
Supporting the finding of meaning

I have learnt you can't force the bud to blossom
Instead flow with the boughs of the tree
As they bend and flex in the winds of new
awareness
And provide the gentle breeze of open questions

Witnessing a more creative, reflective brain
Signals the beginning of spring
Our roles as coaches

Creating the best conditions
For the blossoming to begin

"Massaging my ego – my internal challenge"

ICF code of ethics embedded
Refrain from giving advice
The importance of engaging the whole brain
researched
The coach's role
Helping the client engage the emotive and
sensory parts

But what about my ego
Wanting to be seen as expert
When the client asks what do you think?
Ah! I think my expertise is recognised
Ethically I do not give advice as a coach
But occasionally I fall into the trap
And my ego takes centre stage

So I reflect on my ongoing learning process
Witness my ego internally
Understand my need to be seen as expert
Reflecting in action
And setting my need aside

Instead focusing on supporting my client
Think for themselves
Developing their own solutions

Rejoicing in their growth internally
And the role I play

"Metamorphosis"

Cocoon tight
Learning and growth
Breaking free
Tight constraints fall away
Wings stretching
I feel myself warming as I bask

Freedom to fly
Responsibility to deliver
The colours I see are rich and clear

Punching my way out of my skin
Reframing who I am
Expanding into the skin of the new me
The authentic me

I know this me
Humble, playful, creative
A generosity of spirit
A willingness to be vulnerable
In my new skin
I welcome him
I feel the joy of acceptance
I sense an inner calmness

I vision my growth ahead
In a skin which moves and stretches with me
I know and welcome this me
I have been waiting for you

"Patterns"

I am curious
Curious about the patterns my clients bring
Unhelpful sleeping patterns
Caused by perceived work pressure
Why is it that so many clients are coming with
this pattern?

What does this say about me as a coach?
What am I holding here?
How do I feel about sleep patterns, stress and
alcohol?
How does this impact how I coach?

Has our relationship come to a place where they
can be open?
About what was previously hidden?
Is it about the type of organisations I am working
in?
Or does it say something about society?
Is there a boundary issue here?
As alcohol plays a part in their current solution

What I know to be true is

I don't judge clients for their patterns
I feel privileged that they share them so openly
I want to support them in finding a solution

But am I up to it?
Am I misjudging boundaries?
Are my views regarding alcohol impacting my
ability to coach effectively?

All these questions are worthy of self-reflection
And bringing to supervision

"The playful elephant"

How am I when I am showing mastery?
I am an elephant
Stoic in my resolve

My ethics, standards and competency
Provide a solid foundation
I am wise and understand my territory
Which I patrol with great regularity

My ears open to understanding clients' stories
Actively listening with a large sense of presence
I explore and stretch myself
In a close and supportive community

I am learning how to be playful
In my ever-evolving practice

Rolling in the waterhole of creativity
My symbolistic trunk spraying
And spreading my sense of fun

I march forward steadily
With a generosity of spirit
To support others on their journey
Keep it up two, three, four
The message to myself

There are generic references to the use of reflective poetry as a means of helping students develop their self-reflective capacities within the context of international social work practice and the nursing profession (Furman 2008, Johns 2013). There is also evidence from a research project on the student nurse's perspective of reflective writing and poetry writing which concludes that poetry writing gives students the opportunity for freedom of expression, personal satisfaction and a closer connection with their patients, which the more formal approach to reflective writing does not offer.

The journal of poetry therapy (http://www.poetrytherapy.org/links.poetry.html) has some useful resources and this quote from Graham-Pole seeks to define the power of reflective poetry in therapy. *"Creativity is great medicine for all, both the creator and the one who experiences it. It prevents disease and promotes wellness. It is not indulgence, it is fundamental to medical practice"* (2000).

I have not been able to find any specific evidence of using

poetry as a method of self-reflection in the coaching profession. However, I do have evidence from personal experience that it can be an approach which supports tapping into the unconscious mind and that it can be a freeing, energising and challenging method of self-reflection.

Reflective challenge

Make some space immediately after a coaching or supervision session to reflect using the medium of poetry. Don't overthink the words, instead focus on engaging your creativity and give permission to yourself to just be in a reflective space and see what comes up for you.

Reflective drawing

Within the visual arts world a journal is used to capture visual language and drawn images which are related to reflecting on issues and challenges. These images can be invented or collected from the environment surrounding you. Reflective drawing can also be used to consider a hypothetical challenge or dilemma. Doodling, graffiti and abstract drawings are other alternative forms which can be used to express thoughts and feelings. Rudolf Arnheim developed the idea of concept drawings where visual imagery containing lines, arrows and shapes are used to communicate ideas. Arnheim describes the process as concepts taking shape where the resulting images include both emotional and cognitive themes which indicate personal interpretations of 'lifeworld' experiences.

Another approach is automatic drawing which comes from surrealism. It is described as a way of expressing the subconscious. The automatic drawing style starts with allowing your hand to move wherever it wants to go on the paper free of rational control. It is argued that the drawing produced can be attributed in part to the subconscious mind and can reveal what could have been suppressed. The technique uses the unconscious mind to draw out issues, events or experiences without the starting point of a particular idea or topic. Some surrealist artists have stated that 'automatic drawing' was not absolutely automatic and that it involved both the conscious and unconscious mind. The reasoning provided for the conscious involvement was in order for the painting to be either visually acceptable or understandable. *"...Masson admitted that his 'automatic' imagery involved a two-fold process of unconscious and conscious activity..."* (Montagu 2002, p15).

An example of automatic drawing by Mark Bisson (2016)

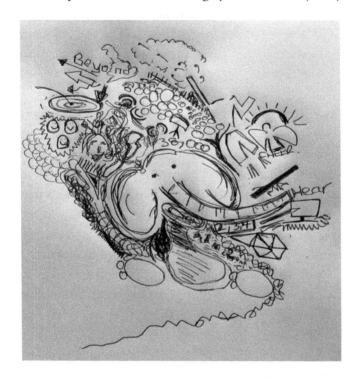

For coaches and supervisors who have a visual lead representational system, drawing can be a very powerful method of self-reflection. Drawing can be used to look back, reflect on current reality and to vision ahead. I have used drawing to provide a symbolistic image of something which has blocked me and to articulate how I want something to be in the future. You don't need to be a talented artist to benefit from this approach. However you articulate your images, the importance and power in using drawing to self-reflect is that they are your images that tell a story and have meaning for you. For some people, a seemingly ritualistic destroying of an image reinforces a learning. For others, images they created are given prominence in their study or office as a reminder of the journey they have been on and the learning they have achieved.

I have also used museums and art galleries to support my self-reflection as advocated by Western (2012). The approach I use is to choose a gallery randomly and then wander until I see a painting which means something to me in the context of the topic or dilemma I am reflecting on. I then stand or sit and reflect whilst looking at the painting and allow space for the messages from the painting to populate my conscious mind. Sometimes I draw my version of the painting in my notebook and write my learnings alongside it. Western advocates *"using the art and the space to reflect on how you locate yourself in the world of work"* (2012, p145). An alternative would be to reflect on how you locate yourself in your coaching practice. This may raise questions of identity, aspiration, family and social expectations, inhibitions and physicality.

Here are some other questions to reflect on as you walk around the gallery. Some are from Western (2012, p146) and others are those I have developed using Western's questions as a catalyst:

- What makes you feel located or grounded as a coach or supervisor?
- What makes you uncomfortable or alienated?
- What pictures/art do you distance yourself from and walk away from. What makes you do that?

- What feelings does the art work bring up in you?
- What memories or shadows from your past are resurrected?
- What associations are you making with the art work?
- What is your body saying?
- What connections are you making?
- What are you left curious about?
- What are you left preoccupied by?

Of course you don't need to use all of the questions. However, you may want to reflect on which questions you could be avoiding.

Rich pictures is another approach which appeals to those with a visual leaning to their self-reflection. The approach I use involves using images and words from a variety of magazines to produce a visual collage which is representative of the topic I am reflecting on and my learnings. The process of searching through the magazines to find the right images provides a reflective space and the collage tells a visual story which represents the reflection undertaken.

Reflective challenge

Choose a method of visual reflection and produce a visual image which is representative of your current coaching and supervision practice. Then visualise what would represent your coaching or supervision practice after a set period of time into the future. Then produce a visual image or images to reflect how you want to be as coach or supervisor at the end of the time period you have selected. You could also produce images of milestones you want to achieve.

Sand play

Margaret Lowenfeld developed sand play therapy in the 1930's in her work with vulnerable children. She identified that the projective play approach allowed the child to explore their own world in what Amas describes as a *"safe and trusting relationship with an adult in any way they wished, much as they would in natural play"* (2007, p10). Whilst it had its starting point in child therapy, eminent Jungian and Gestalt therapists recognised the benefits of using the technique with adults. Stevens (2004) refers to the potential of the technique for bringing unconscious material into the conscious world.

The sand play technique of reflection is now used commonly in the social work profession to support direct interaction with vulnerable children and young people in the development of life stories. One exercise titled projective play is particularly relevant to self-reflection in the coaching profession as a group or individual activity. The exercise involves the use of a large wooden box or plastic tray as well as other materials including Play-Doh, sand, water and other objects including small plastic and metal figures, jewels and string.

Each person participating is invited to build a landscape representing their professional or practice world and then they explore it narratively with other coaches. My experience of this technique is that it has the ability to draw out dynamics, both within coaching or supervision relationships and in wider organisational and cultural contexts. The exercise can create learning insights relating to ethics, deep-held beliefs and the role of power in coaching or supervision relationships.

A word of caution from my experience. Sand play exercises need to be carefully facilitated by someone who is trained and experienced in the use of the technique. On the subject of facilitation, De Domenico says that:

> "Sand play evokes very deep realities. It cuts across many familial and cultural taboos as it activates the deep, primordial integrative forces of the psyche. Whether an educator, a trained expressive or play therapist or whether an accomplished verbal, behavioural, or cognitive clinician, each sand play facilitator needs to use the sand tray for his/her own personal growth and development before integrating the tool into the play – and consultation room" (1995, p7).

Amas (2007) undertook research with social work practitioners which evidenced that sand play:

> "providing it is set up correctly, is a creative space for the student/practitioner to explore practice" and that "The making of the sand landscape helps students/practitioners construct an understanding and potentially resolve issues or find deeper meanings and contexts for their work" (2007, p9).

Reflective metaphor

The ability to reflect on practice using metaphors can support understanding of the assumptions, judgements and beliefs that are contained within them. Metaphors have a richness and provide a lot of information in a small number of words. They also have a tendency to generate strong emotions in us and are therefore potentially powerful tools for new learning. The vividness thesis suggests that metaphors provide a more memorable learning due to the imagery or concreteness or vividness of the experience conjured up by the metaphorical vehicle (Inglese and Rigotti, 2011). Ortony defines metaphors as having "*a possibly unique role in helping the acquisition of new knowledge*". This happens through their use to "*transfer learning and understanding from what is well known to what is less known in a vivid and memorable way*" (1993, p580). Using metaphors reflectively enables us to make a connection between symbolism and the learning we take through their use. In this way, the metaphor helps embed the learning in our conscious brain in a format which is easier for us to understand. MacCormac refers to the use of metaphors in providing clarity to the unknown which then provides an opportunity for the creation of new insight. He posits that "*To describe the unknown, we must resort to concepts that we know and understand, and that is the essence of a metaphor, an unusual juxtaposition of the familiar with the unfamiliar*" (1990, p9).

Examples of reflective metaphors include:

- Education policy is removing the oxygen supply from the classroom
- Time is a thief
- It feels like I am hitting my head against a brick wall
- I am going round and round in circles
- The monster inside of me keeps escaping
- We are up against it this year
- Which branch of the organisation are you in?
- Coaching supervision is growing
- I need to build my skills

Ortony (1975) states that the role of a metaphor is as a tool for overcoming active memory limitations in the use of spoken language. One of the findings from research undertaken by Lawley and Tomkins (2000) evidences that when a person decides to make changes to their metaphors the actions and decisions they take also alter. However, there are limitations when using metaphors as a tool for self-reflection.

Lawley and Tomkins go on to say that:

> *"Metaphors illuminate some aspects of an experience while leaving other aspects in the shadows. Therefore they are a source of creativity and at the same time they constrain our ways of thinking to that which makes sense within the metaphor. This influences the meaning and importance we attach to the original experience, the way it fits with other experiences, and the actions we take as a result"* (2006).

Reflective challenge

Think about a metaphor that means something to you in your coaching or supervision practice. It could relate to a problem, dilemma or pattern you have identified. It could be a metaphor which you feel is a reflection of you as a coach or supervisor. Lawley and Tomkins (2006) suggest that whatever a person says, sees, hears, feels or does, as well as what they imagine, can be used to comprehend and reason through metaphor. What is the metaphor saying to you? What does it say about how you practise? What learning do you take from the metaphor?

Reflective dialogue

This approach is used in a group setting. The process involves coaches sharing their own thoughts and feelings on a topic or dilemma and then each member of the group undertaking self-reflection on their reaction to the responses of the other participating coaches (Gray 2007). The dialogue serves a dual purpose. To learn from each other and to critically reflect on the assumptions, values, beliefs and judgements being made which sit behind the thinking and feelings which have often resided in the individual coach at an unconscious level.

In more informal group settings it is possible for each participant to bring a piece of practice to work on in two stages: a reflective awareness stage and a linking with practice stage. The aim of group reflective dialogue is to develop changes to practice as a result of reflections on fundamental assumptions and, in NLP terms, the coach's existing map of the world. The process, however, functions in different ways, according to the meaning of the topic or dilemma which is raised for the person themselves. This will also depend on how it is theorised and understood and of course, on what types of fundamental assumptions are revealed for each person.

Participants bring a description of the topic from their practice. Group members help them reflect by using a set of questions. For example:

> *"What does your practice imply about…? What were you assuming when…? How did you influence the situation through your presence, perceptions, body language, interpretations, assumptions? What were your beliefs about power in the situation and where did they come from? What perspectives are missing? What language patterns have you used and what do they imply? What is your own thinking and what is the result of power relations e.g. gendered, cultural, structural?" (Fook 2006, p6).*

Scripts relating to reflective models

Gibbs' reflective cycle

In part one I referred to Gibbs' reflective cycle – the cycle involving six elements with a number of prompt questions in each element to support your self-reflection. The cycle can be used to reflect on a specific incident or event. I have amended the questions to suit the professional coaching and supervision context as follows:

Description

- What happened? Don't make judgements yet try to draw conclusions. Simply describe.
- Using specific and relevant detail, provide a concise description of what happened.

Feelings

- What were your reactions and feelings? Again, don't move on to analysing these yet.
- How did you feel and what did you think prior to the session?
- How did you feel and what did you think during the session?
- How did you react during the session?
- How did you feel and what did you think after the session?

Evaluation

- What was good or bad about the experience? Make value judgements.
- How did the session end?

Analysis

- What sense can you make of the situation? Bring in ideas from outside the experience to help you."
- "What was really going on?
- What didn't go well and what did this lead to in the session?
- What could I have done to avoid this?
- What went well in the session and what did this lead to in the session?
- How was my contribution useful to the client?

Conclusions (general)

- What can be concluded, in a general sense, from these experiences and the analyses you have undertaken?
- What did I learn about my current knowledge or level of practice (strengths and weaknesses)?

Conclusions (specific)

- What should or could I have done differently?
- What stopped me from doing this?
- What did I learn about myself during the experience (positive and/or negative)?
- What can be concluded about my own specific, unique, personal situation or way of working?

Personal action plans

- What are you going to do differently in this type of situation next time?
- What steps are you going to take on the basis of what you have learnt?
- What areas which I consider to be strengths can I become even better at?

Reflective challenge

Use the Gibbs' model to reflect on a positive experience from a coaching or supervision session. Identify your learnings from focusing on what went well. How did this support the development of your practice?

Johns' model of structured reflection

I have amended the latest version of the MSR model to reflect how it can be used from the coaching profession's perspective:

Preparatory phase

- Bring the mind home (this could include a mindfulness exercise).

Descriptive phase

- Focus on a description of a session, pattern or dilemma which seems significant in some way (you may decide to provide a balance between situations or topics which were affirming and those that were problematic).

Reflective phase

- What issues are significant to pay attention to?
- How was the client feeling and what caused this feeling?
- How was I feeling and what made me feel that way?
- What was I trying to achieve and did I respond effectively?
- What were the consequences of my approach for the client and myself?
- To what extent did I act ethically and in tune with my values?
- What knowledge did or might have informed me?
- How does this situation/experience/pattern/dilemma connect with previous experience?
- What assumptions governed how I coached?
- What factors influenced the way I felt, thought and responded to this particular situation/experience/pattern/dilemma?

Anticipatory phase

- How might I reframe the situation/experience/pattern/dilemma in order to coach/supervise more effectively?

- What could be the consequences of adopting a different approach in the future?
- What factors might constrain me from adopting a new approach?
- How do I now feel about this experience?

Insight phase

What insights have I gained?

The following are two examples of how coaches and supervisors can use the model with questions to prompt reflection. I have adapted both in order that they reflect my perception of the needs of self-reflection in coaching whilst staying true to the model:

Model for Structured Reflection – adapted from Johns (2000) Example 1:

Looking in

- Find a space to focus on self
- Pay attention to your thoughts and emotions
- Write down these thoughts and emotions

Looking out

- Write a reflective description of the situation
- What issues seem significant?

Aesthetics

- What was I trying to achieve?
- What prompted me to respond as I did?
- What were the consequences for myself and my client?
- How do I believe my client was feeling?
- How did I know this?

Personal

- What prompted me to feel the way I did within this situation?

Ethics

- Did I act for the best?
- What factors were influencing me?
- What knowledge did or could have informed me?

Reflexivity

- How does this situation relate to previous experiences?
- How could I have handled this better?
- What would have been the consequences of alternative actions?
- How do I feel now about the experience?
- How can I support myself and others better in the future?

Johns' structured model of reflection cue questions
Example 2:

Description of the experience

Phenomenon – describe the here and now experience

Causal – what essential factors contributed to this experience?

Context – what are the significant background factors to this experience?

Clarifying – what are the key processes (for reflection) in this experience?

Reflection

- What was I trying to achieve?
- What prompted me to ask the questions I did?
- What were the consequences of my actions for:
  - o Myself?
  - o The client?
  - o The wider organisational/political context?
- How did I feel about this experience when it was happening?
- How do I perceive what the client felt about it?
- How do I know this?

Influencing factors

- What internal factors influenced me?
- What external factors influenced me?
- What sources of knowledge did/should have influenced me?
- Could I have dealt with the situation better?
- What choices did I have?
- What would be the consequences of these choices?

Learning

- How do I feel now about this experience?
- How have I made sense of this experience in light of past experiences and future practice?
- How has this experience changed my ways of knowing and awareness?

Reflective challenge

Choose a set of cue questions from the examples provided and reflect on a coaching or supervision session you have undertaken in the last week. What worked with the prompt questions? What didn't work? Consider the reasons why these questions did or didn't work for you.

Mezirow's transformative learning theory

The following is my adaptation of the seven levels of reflectivity with question prompts for use in your self-reflection. In essence, the template I have provided is an activity in meaning-making.

1. Disorientating dilemma

- Describe the event/situation/session
- You could use storytelling or imagery to support your description.

2. Self-examination of effect

- What are you aware of feeling? Describe the feeling.

3. Critical assessment of assumptions

- What does it mean to you to feel like this?
- What advice did you give and are you giving yourself?
- What is your interpretation of what happened?
- What was your intention?

4. Exploration of new roles

- How would you prefer this to be different? (Reframe leading to action)
- What new expectation do you have of yourself?

- When this begins to happen in your practice what will be different about you?

5. Planning a course of action (recognising the potential blockers)

- What are you aware of that could stop this from happening?
- What are the risks and dangers to avoid?
- What are the benefits of staying as you are in your practice?
- What is one small step you can take that will start you on your journey of being different?

6. Acquiring knowledge and skills for implementation

- What will you need to know, accomplish and overcome for this to occur consistently in your practice?

7. Trying out new roles

- How will you know you are on track?

Reflective challenge

Try this model out with a change you want to make in your practice using a real situation from your past as a catalyst for the exploration. Make a note of your learnings, what meaning-making has taken place and the action you now want to take.

Rolfe's reflective model

I have adapted the prompt questions in Rolfe's cyclical model. As you use this model, you may find that you develop your own set of prompt questions which work for you.

What – describe the situation: achievements, consequences, responses, feelings and problems.

- ... is the problem/difficulty/reason for being stuck/ reason for feeling bad/reason we don't get on?
- ... was my role in the situation?
- ... was I trying to achieve?
- ... actions did I take?
- ... was the response of my client?
- ... were the consequences for the client and myself or others?
- ... feelings did it evoke in the client and myself and how do I know this?
- ... was good/bad about the experience?

So what – discuss what has been learnt: learning about self, relationships, models, attitudes, cultures, actions, thoughts, understanding and improvements.

- ... does this tell me/teach me/imply/mean about me/our relationship/my attitudes/my client's attitudes?

- … was going through my mind?
- … did I base my approach on?
- … other knowledge can I bring to the situation?
- … could/should I have done to make it better?
- … is my new understanding of the situation?
- … broader issues arise from the situation?

Now what – identify what needs to be done in order to: improve future outcomes and develop learning

- … do I need to do in order to make things better/ stop being stuck/improve my practice/resolve the situation/feel better/get on better etc., etc.?
- … broader issues need to be considered if this action is to be successful?
- … might be the consequences of this action?

Adapted from: Rolfe, G., Freshwater, D., Jasper, M. (2001) *Critical reflection in nursing and the helping professions: a user's guide*.

Reflective challenge

Try using this model with a current challenge you have in your coaching or supervision practice. Then use one of the other cyclical models and reflect on the differences and similarities in your responses to the questions in each model.

Ending coaching and supervision relationships – an
opportunity for reflection

The conclusion of a coaching or supervision relationship
provides an opportunity for reflection and feedback from
clients. As well as focusing on the specific dynamics of
the relationship, it can also be a space where feedback
can be sought on our coaching or supervision practice.
To prompt a deeper level of reflection beyond descriptive
stories, I developed the following template which
includes prompt questions for use with my supervision
clients. You could ask clients to complete the template
in advance of the final session so, in Schön's words,
they have the opportunity to 'reflect on action' from the
balcony.

Coaching supervision feedback template

Name of supervisee   Date

Building rapport by putting some of myself as interviewer into
the session, possibly by raising similar or different experiences
(Arksey and Knight 1999).

Did I build rapport with you and, if so, what was the
impact from your perspective as supervisee?

What impact/ influence did I have as coach supervisor?

Hawkins (Bachkirova, Cox and Clutterbuck 2014, p394) state that coach supervision has three elements:

- Coaching the coach on their coaching – Resourcing
- Mentoring the coach on their development in the profession – Developmental
- Providing an external perspective to ensure quality of practice – Qualitative

What evidence do you have that I coached you on your coaching practice?

How did I mentor you on your development in the coaching profession?

What evidence do you have of my external perspective supporting you in ensuring the quality of your practice?

Notes to take during interview, Easterby-Smith (2002, p123):

1. What was the relationship like between coach supervisor and supervisee?

Closed									Open
1	2	3	4	5	6	7	8	9	10

2. What was the attitude of the supervisor?

Disengaged									Engaged
1	2	3	4	5	6	7	8	9	10

3. What is your level of confidence in me as coach supervisor?

Unconfident									Very confident
1	2	3	4	5	6	7	8	9	10

The following is an example of a completed coach supervision feedback form:

Coach supervision feedback
Supervisor   Mark Bisson
Supervisee   J A
Time period of supervision: January 2015 to July 2015

What were your goals and support needs from supervision?

I am starting out on my coaching experience whilst training for the qualification. As part of the training, I have to do a certain amount of direct coaching and supervision. What I wanted from the supervision was someone who could both challenge and support me in my transition and adoption of the coaching skills I had learnt, in a practical and not academic way.

What progress have you made on the goals and support needs you identified?

I have made significant progress and with Mark we have been able to tackle a number of the key issues in my transition. I am still learning and developing as a coach, but one of the things I have grown to understand is the value of the supervisor role in both developing and having someone with the relevant experience who you can ask for advice and who will constructively question your thinking.

Please provide feedback in the three areas which Proctor (1986) uses to define the nature of supervision:

• normative – the supervisor accepts (or more accurately shares with the supervisee) responsibility for ensuring that the supervisee's work is professional and ethical, operating within whatever codes, laws and organisational norms apply:

Does not share									shares responsibility
1	2	3	4	5	6	7	8	9	10

Narrative to support score:

I have discussed a number of ethical areas with Mark, and we spent some time unravelling the role of a coach within an organisation and what the 'practical' boundaries to this would be that would support effective coaching whilst understanding and working within the organisational dynamic. Mark supported greatly in helping me become comfortable with my understanding of the role. I also had a specific situation with a coachee I felt was effectively 'uncoachable' and required a different approach; being able to discuss this fully before finalising what was needed and what to say to the coachee was very important.

- formative – the supervisor acts to provide feedback or direction that will enable the supervisee to develop the skills, theoretical knowledge, personal attributes and so on that will mean the supervisee becomes an increasingly competent practitioner.

Not acting									provides excellent feedback and direction
1	2	3	4	5	6	7	8	9	10

Narrative to support score:

One example that was especially key was when Mark reviewed my own detailed analysis of my coaching (a word by word analysis); with Mark I was able to take this to a deeper level, progressing further my own development in saying less, holding the silence and the pause, and not leading, even subtly. However, in this exercise he also helped me understand the difference between the feeling and the thinking modes of a conversation. By understanding and using this knowledge I have become a much more effective and aware coach.

- supportive (Proctor calls this restorative) – the supervisor is there to listen, support, confront the supervisee when the inevitable personal issues, doubts and insecurities arise – and when client issues are 'picked up' by the supervisee:

Does not listen or support									Listens and supports
1	2	3	4	5	6	7	8	9	10

Narrative to support score:

As above, assistance in the role and different performance of an internal coach and a specific tricky situation was very important. In addition, one of the things I found very useful was that in every session I felt I left with another 'tool', be it knowledge or something I could use or research. I felt comfortable and supported discussing my weaknesses and concerns about my own abilities and the necessary change from a directive management style to a coaching position; the answers were not given, but I was helped to explore them and get there.

Describe two attributes you have valued about my supervision:

The honesty and the connection I felt: I believed my supervisor was genuinely engaged on the 'journey of change' I was going through and this made me feel comfortable opening and talking through the areas I was finding tricky.

The practical support tips: I was able to use the tools I was shown, they were practical and useable at the stage I was at. The explanations and 'tricks' have helped me move to a more sensory approach, taking in more about the coachee, their body language, what they did not say and starting to develop and utilise my use of self, rather than focusing solely on what was said.

Describe two things I should work on to improve my supervision practice:

I sometimes found the sessions slow to get into the swing with the opening 10-15 mins on the 'supervisor questions'. I also found these sometimes a bit repetitive with me feeling the same answers were relevant to different questions, so this part of the session sometimes felt a bit too formulaic.

Whilst I understand the value of Skype and for us to work together there would have been no other way, it also has its limitations and I sense a face-to-face session would have been more powerful. This was not possible so need to think how to use the Skype medium to gain advantages that would replace what is lost by not having a face-to-face. I am not sure what the answer to this is; I sense it is somehow using the technology to be able to share/participate/engage in other ways to compensate for the lack of face-to-face.

Adapted from Proctor, Brigid (1986) *Supervision: A co-operative exercise in accountability* in M Marken & M Payne (eds) *Enabling and Ensuring: Supervision in Practice* National Youth Bureau/Council for Education and Training in Youth and Community Work.

Reflective challenge

When a coaching or supervision relationship reaches a natural ending, include in the final session an opportunity for you and the coachee/supervisee to collaborate in reflecting on the relationship, the journey and your learnings.

The use of mindfulness and presence

As coaches and supervisors, we can sometimes struggle to maintain a state of presence in our sessions. Practising mindfulness can support us in how we develop and maintain focus within the coaching session and to support our emotional detachment.

Mindfulness is a practice which emanates from Buddhist and other meditative traditions. Kabat-Zinn (1990) states that these traditions teach the art of 'non-doing' to facilitate absorbing reality 'as is'. Mindfulness supports the creation of conscious attention and awareness of the moment. We all have our own map of the world, although Miller (1956) describes this as an illusion based on our own individual experiences. At any one moment we are able to process between five and nine pieces of information when we have several million available to us.

A definition of mindfulness is *"A mental state achieved by focusing one's awareness on the present moment while calmly acknowledging and accepting one's feelings, thoughts, and bodily sensations"* (oxforddictionaries.com).

Murdoch and Arnold, referring to mindfulness, describe the impact as tapping into *"… the silence that quietens us down, it enables us to go deeper into the soul of our sessions. It gives us the capability to 'hold' the different parts of the system and to be acutely aware of what is often not said"* (2013, p38).

Being in a state of mindfulness provides an opportunity to temporarily remove the restrictions of our own mental processes and models. Passmore and Marianetti refer to this is as *"a way of investigating reality that challenges our sense of safety derived by the illusion and the safety of 'knowing"* (2013, p132). To be effective in the use of mindfulness requires ongoing practice. My own experience is based on starting with relatively small durations and building up over time. There are a number of apps which support this learning through mindfulness teaching and music. Buddhify and Headspace are two examples.

Research on mindfulness evidences that there are four key elements in play when being mindful. These are awareness, attention (Brown and Ryan 2003), time (Kabat-Zinn 1990) and acceptance (Gunaratana 1993).

Passmore and Marianetti define the four elements in the following way:

"Awareness is the brain's ability to constantly monitor and recognise internal and external systems and stimuli. Attention is the brain's ability to focus the awareness to a specific phenomenon and so increasing the sensitivity to it. Time refers to 'the now'; the only place where we exist, experience and act. Acceptance represents our ability to let go and to be non-judgemental; our ability to observe and absorb reality 'as is', without embarrassment, satisfaction or disappointment" (2013, p131).

Previously, I spoke of practising reflection 'in action'. In order to do so requires us as coaches and supervisors to be present in the moment. I believe that being in a state of mindfulness supports us in optimising our ability to reflect in action. One approach I have undertaken prior to a coaching session is to run a short mindfulness meditation to support me in being in a state of readiness for the session. This involves a combination of focusing in on my breathing and bodily state. The outcomes I have experienced have included clearing of thoughts and feelings from the day so far as well as releasing stress and reduction in feelings of anxiety.

There has been some criticism of using mindfulness which centres on a view that a practitioner being mindful results in them becoming a disassociated observer. Murdoch and Arnold agree that "*a distorted application of mindfulness can lead to an apparently emotionless, sitting beyond and outside the messiness of human interaction*" (2013, p129). My own experience is that mindfulness which is authentic comes from the heart and that it is being from this place which ensures that we are aware and sense the feelings of our clients. There are obvious links here with the principles of emotional intelligence and our ability as practitioners to understand and listen to our emotional states.

Our breath is the easiest part of our human mechanics to bring our attention to in order to develop the habit of mindfulness. Stern describes the effect of the routine practice of focusing on our breath as having the impact of creating a presence in ourselves which allows us to be mindful of *"whatever is in the awareness now, during the moment being lived"* (2004, p32). Shohet reinforces this by stating that when breath is the focus *"I am more alive to the moment, more present, more in the here and now"* (2008, p73). This focus helps us to be more in tune with alterations and presence of our feelings, perceptions and to our physical sensations.

Here is an exercise which I have developed and continue to use for myself and with coachees and supervisees.

Mindful Breathing

This exercise should be done sitting. Find a straight-backed chair and, as you sit down, notice the chair against your back and the sensation of sitting. Put your feet flat on the floor don't cross your legs and keep your knees apart. All you have to do is focus on your breath for two minutes. It's up to you whether you close your eyes or leave them open.

First, notice your feet and how they feel as they meet the floor and then slowly work your way up your body noticing your legs, bottom and how you are located in your chair. Then move slowly up to your arms, your chest then your neck and your head. With each part of your body notice the sensations and feelings emanating from them as you sit.

Now start to focus on your breath and breathe in and out slowly at a pace which works for you and count the number of seconds in and out. Initially, don't try to alter your breathing pattern, just count it in and out. Then focus on lengthening the in-breath and out-breath phases and, if it's comfortable, try to increase to six seconds for each phase. As you breathe in notice your chest rise. You could even put your hand on your abdomen and, as you breathe out, let your breath flow effortlessly and calmly back into the atmosphere.

To start with, it will be natural for your mind to wander off. Simply notice these thoughts and let them be and bring yourself back to watching your breath as it enters your body and fills you with life and then watch as it works its way back up and out of your body.

Once you have mastered this exercise it is available for you to use in a variety of settings in your life. Many mindfulness practitioners describe it as less of a technique and more of a way of living. This is amplified in this quote from Jon Kabat-Zinn.

"It's not that mindfulness is the 'answer' to all life's problems. Rather it is that all life's problems can be seen more clearly through the lens of a clear mind" (1990, p25).

Relaxation exercises

If you have difficulty relaxing, find somewhere quiet to sit or lie and recall a place or a time when you felt calm and at peace. Take time to remember what it was like to be there and really notice what you felt, saw and heard at the time and how this impacted your body. Notice the colours, the sounds and the feelings this gave you. Allow yourself time to be in this familiar place or moment from your past and recognise that you can go there whenever you want.

Another exercise involves viewing something from the natural environment around us. This could be looking out of a window or locating yourself in the environment. Focus in on a detail of a specific element of the environment and explore it. If it was a tree for instance, then really notice the tree, the bark, the branches, the leaves, insects, birds and animals which live in the tree, notice the root system and where it was located. Notice how the tree moves if there is wind, notice how the sun changes the colour and casts shadows. If other thoughts come into your mind allow them to float there and then drift away. Bring yourself back to the place or object. Notice what it is like to be in this calm place and enjoy the freedom.

At the end of these exercises, whenever you are ready bring yourself back into the here and now and slowly open your eyes. Somtimes at this point you may choose to stretch your arms as you acknowledge the calm, mindful space you are in. The exercises can help you prepare for a coaching or supervision session in terms of managing your internal state and ensuring you remain in a place of presence with your client.

The importance of presence in coaching and supervision

The ICF defines presence as *"the ability to be fully conscious and create spontaneous relationships with the client, employing a style that is open, flexible and confident"*. According to existential psychologist, James Bugental, presence calls our attention to how genuinely and completely a person is in a situation rather than standing apart from it as observer, commentator, critic or judge (Bugental J.F.T., 1987). A further definition describes presence as *"a state of awareness, in the moment, characterised by the felt experience of timelessness, connectedness and a larger truth"* (Silsbee 2008, p21).

The full spectrum model also references the importance of mindfulness and presence. Murdoch and Arnold define presence as *"the quality of total engagement and wide but precise awareness of the self and others"* (2013, p121). They go on to argue that *"Who you are is how you supervise"* and define the requirements of an effective supervisor as:

- *Model openness, calmness and authenticity*

- *Demonstrate a level of clarity about ourselves, the supervisee and the supervisee's client that will identify areas of parallel process and transference*

- *Help the supervisee reflect on wider and deeper implications beyond a specific client or situation*

- *Access deep levels of intuition and intuitive wisdom*

- *"Be prepared to operate in a field of not knowing in which knowledge, understanding and wisdom can spontaneously arise"*

Murdoch and Arnold (2013, p122).

Mindfulness and presence contribute towards these abilities in a supervisor by allowing them to hold a whole-field awareness and allow a safe space for challenge to take place. During my academic and experiential learning journey I have become consciously aware of strategies I used to be 'present'. These include positioning of chairs, matching body position and pace/tone of speech. I sometimes recall an anchor of a time in my personal life when I was confident and totally in the moment to elicit a 'present state' where the client is my sole focus rather than my own internal representations.

Being fully present is not only something that we can judge internally from our freedom, from our inner voice and being aware of the environment we are in; our clients will know when we are and when we are not present.

Although this can be difficult to articulate, it revolves around congruity. Clients will sense when you are being silent appropriately and also when a question is asked which has a heart and mind connection. Murdoch and Arnold believe that a possible purpose of presence is to create a space where "... *creativity and insight may manifest. It is not about fixing anything – although solutions may arise*" (2013, p133).

I believe there is a link between presence and being mindful whilst they are clearly not the same thing. Murdoch and Arnold add weight to this view from their own experience which leads them to state that it is possible "... *to be mindfully aware without being present but not possible to be present without being mindfully aware*" (2013, p136). What I take from this is that, in order to be present, your mind and body need to first be in a place of calmness. My view of presence in its purest state is that I am in a place of natural flow, I am relaxed, grounded in the moment and no effort is required. In fact it is effortless.

Reflective challenge

Set some time aside, preferably immediately after the session, to reflect on a coaching or supervision conversation from the perspective of presence? Use the time to answer some or all of the following questions:

- How well did you suppress or isolate your own emotions and cognition?

- Were you aware that you were distracted or drifting? If so, what was the cause?

- How much mindful effort were you making to maintain awareness of self, client and the environment?

- Were there moments or periods where maintaining awareness of self, client and the environment felt effortless?

- How sensitive were you to your own intuition?

- Think about examples of when you were deeply intuitive?

PART THREE

*The role of supervision in
supporting self-reflection*

Establishing the philosophical principles and purpose of coach supervision

Coaching is a relatively new profession and it was only as the new millennium approached that leading authors in the field of coaching began to advocate coach supervision which has its roots in the practice of clinical supervision (Downey 1999, Flaherty 1999). Effective coach supervision creates a safe space for both supervisee and supervisor to work together in partnership to create new awareness and insight for the supervisee. In doing so, the supervisor working at their best connects with their *"wise compassionate observer"* in showing *"unconditional kindliness towards ourselves that is without judgement"* (Murdoch and Arnold 2013, p189). Supervisors need to be mindful that they are working in the service of the supervisee and the organisation within which they are employed. Murdoch and Arnold go on to argue that adopting a psychodynamic approach asks us "... *to look beneath the surface for the conflicting emotions in dynamic tension that may be what is keeping the client stuck"* (2013, p 162).

My definition of coach supervision is *"the act of supporting a coach to widen and deepen their awareness of who and how they are as coach in service of their growth and development to the benefit of the clients they serve"*.

This has the benefit of enhancing the performance of the coach when working with their clients which may be within the organisation where they are employed or working with clients in organisations as an external coach. The benefit of a supervisor external to the organisation is defined from the Network Coach discourse by Western who describes this stance as *"working to align individual and organisational success with social responsibility and sustainability"* (2012, p199). The networked supervisor can bring new ideas and energy to the relationship based on learning from other organisations.

What is coach supervision?

At the core of the principles of coach supervision is that continuing professional and personal development are an inherent part of the learning journey for a professional coach. The International Coaching Federation defines coach supervision as *"the interaction that occurs when a coach periodically brings his or her coaching work experiences to a coaching supervisor in order to engage in reflective dialogue and collaborative learning for the development and benefit of the coach and his or her clients."*

The external support which a supervisor provides helps clarify what is going on in the coaching relationship at both the overt and hidden levels. Coach supervision takes place within a mutually agreed contract with an explicit ethical requirement that links to each coach's 'duty of care' and enables ongoing performance improvement and a consistency of the quality of the coach's practice. Coaches can receive support when they have doubts or insecurities and the supervisor is able to challenge and confront the coach's personal issues. The coach supervisor has a responsibility to ensure that the coach is practising competently and ethically.

CIPD research referencing Bluckert (2004) describes supervision sessions as

> *"… a place for the coach to reflect on the work they are undertaking with another more experienced coach. It has the dual purpose of supporting the continued learning and development of the coach, as well as giving a degree of protection to the person being coached" (2004, p2). Hawkins and Smith argue that coach supervision is "the process by which a coach/mentor/consultant, with the help of a supervisor, can attend to understanding better both the client system and themselves as part of the client-coach system, and by so doing transform their work and develop their craft" (2013, p169).*

The CIPD research paper on coach supervision states that some of the similarities between these definitions include:

- *Supervision is a formal process*
- *It is interpersonal, and can be undertaken one-to-one, in groups or in peer groups*
- *Reflection on client work is central to supervision*
- *Its goals include developing greater coaching competence.*

Supervision in coaching is an emerging field of research. Murdoch and Arnold's (2013) development of the full spectrum model of supervision amplifies the newness and creativity of developing thinking in the realm of coaching supervision. The authors, in describing the theoretical underpinnings of the model, articulate the model's application to practice from adult learning theory, systemics, mindfulness, relationship psychology, neuroscience, quantum physics, advanced dialogue process and spirituality.

There has been some debate, both within and outside the coaching profession, regarding the use of the word 'supervision' in a coaching context. The CIPD research evidenced that *"some individuals and organisations dislike the term 'supervision' since it can create an old-fashioned image of overseeing, monitoring, controlling and policing"* (2006, p3).

The use of the terms 'coach supervisor' and 'coaching supervision' are common, although some organisations have instead described the person and the practice including 'coaching the coach', 'lead coach', 'coach mentor', 'master coach', 'meta-coaching' or 'reflective practice'.

The main elements of coach supervision

Hawkins (Bachkirova, Cox and Clutterbuck 2014, p394) goes on to argue that coach supervision has three elements:

- Coaching the coach on their coaching – Resourcing
- Mentoring the coach on their development in the profession – Developmental
- Providing an external perspective to ensure quality of practice – Qualitative

These elements mirror the three functions suggested by Kadushin (1992) for social work supervision in the 1970s and those that Proctor put forward in the field of counselling (Proctor 1988). Hawkins refers to both being confining to their professional fields with Kadushin (1992) focusing on the role of the supervisor, while Proctor focused on the benefits to the supervisee. Therefore Hawkins decided to develop the elements described above.

The importance of supervision in supporting reflective learning and practice

The eminent thought leader on coach supervision Peter Hawkins (Bachkirova, Cox and Clutterbuck 2014, p394) describes coach supervision as a place of reflection where *"the creation of new understanding and new practice"* takes place. The power of reflective learning emanates from the supervisor's ability to support a supervisee in becoming reflective a practitioner. Doing so effectively provides a space where blind spots such as transference and parallel processes can be identified and actions planned and progressed.

My belief is that choosing coaching as my profession brings with it accountability and responsibility for my own lifelong learning journey to continuously reflect on and improve my practice. I owe it to my clients and the organisations they work for and to myself to be the best that I can be. Although it is possible to self-reflect on our practice, the power and value of coach supervision is in the challenge and support it provides in a safe environment. Therefore, the definition of coaching supervision which I subscribe to and which most closely aligns with my beliefs is from Hawkins and Shohet who state that supervision *"... can be a very important part of taking care of oneself, staying open to new learning, and an indispensable part of the helper's wellbeing, ongoing self-development, self-awareness and commitment to professional development"* (2012, p6).

The importance of self-reflection as a coach is referred to by Patterson (Murdoch and Arnold 2013) who indicates that *"by becoming reflective practitioners we ensure that we engage wholeheartedly in our own learning, unfolding stories of personal and professional development towards becoming more and more of who we truly are"* (2013, p118). This statement resonates with me as I have found that my own path to becoming a coach supervisor has been a journey of reflecting on the stories I have told myself about my past. I have reframed them as a result of new insight from my own self-reflective process. The result is that I have more inner contentment and humility in my coach supervision practice. I now believe that previously my own stories were impacting my practice negatively in terms of the anxieties I had playing out internally. This, in turn, impacted on my ability to be present with a client. Murdoch and Arnold provide advice about anxieties which really supported my progress in this respect. They suggest that "*If we focus on our own anxieties and constantly wonder if we are 'good enough', as supervisors we will stifle our growth. Instead we should focus on the incredible learning journey that supervision provides*" (2013, p64). It is this change in mindset which has helped me on my journey of exploration and transformation as a coach supervisor.

Resnick and Estrup (2000, p122) describe the purpose of supervision from a Gestalt therapy perspective as multidimensional:

* *to help the therapist understand his/her client better at both the content and process levels*
* *to help the therapist become more aware of his/her own reactions and responses to the client (actual and counter-transferential)*
* *to understand the dynamics of how the therapist and client are interacting – from both a clinical and a theoretical perspective*
* *to look at the therapist's interventions and the consequences of these interventions*
* *to learn and compare theories of psychotherapy*
* *to explore other ways of working (other models of psychotherapy) with this and other similar client situations*
* *to both validate (support) and challenge the therapist.*

Hawkins (Bachkirova, Cox and Clutterbuck 2014, p394) indicates that there is much to learn from the helping professions in terms of supervision but that it is important that the coaching profession *"develops its own approach and methodology for supervision which, while learning from what has been developed elsewhere, can address the challenge of coaching having multiple stakeholders"* (2014, p392).

Research conducted for the CIPD by the Bath Consultancy (2008) reinforces this point. The research argues that the published work regarding theories and models utilised in coach supervision is limited and that this is in part because *"coaching supervisors are often drawn from psychology, psychotherapy or counselling backgrounds, where supervision has been established longer"*. The research suggests that *"until the coaching community develops its own definitions, models and theories of supervision, the practice will be limited and coaching supervision will remain 'dressed in borrowed clothes"*, these being the theories and models which emanate from psychology, psychotherapy and counselling. The research (CIPD) argues that this has created three supervision approaches:

- *psychological case work – focusing on understanding the psychology of the coaching client and how to work with it*
- *coaching the coach – focusing on the coach rather than on their coaching*
- *managerial supervision – focusing on fixing problems and resolving difficulties.*

The CIPD research indicated that coach supervision should develop its own models so that reflective learning focuses on:

- *better understanding the coach's clients and their organisational context*
- *exploring coaching relationships*
- *developing ways of improving coaching and coaching interventions*
- *contributing to the coach's continuing professional development*
- *attending to the 'live' relationship between coach and supervisor and the ways this might be paralleling the coaching session dynamics*
- *ensuring the coach is supported and resourced to manage coaching work within their capability.*

Research undertaken by Casement (1985) evidenced that newly-qualified therapists relied too much on their supervisor for advice and direction. I also found this was the case for me in the early months of supervision practice. I would identify issues and dilemmas to bring to supervision but did not undertake self-reflection to identify new insights about myself or to consider identifying my own solutions. It was when I was challenged by my supervisor to undertake my own self-reflection in advance of supervision sessions that the quality and depth of my self-reflection began to improve. In Casement's words I was beginning to get a sense of my own 'internal supervisor'. The parallel process is that, as a supervisor, I am encouraging the client towards self-knowledge. Obtaining the ability for self-evaluation and more belief in my own judgement has had the impact of turning down the volume on my inner critic.

Rickard (2011) describes experience of using Schön's model of reflection in action and reflection on action to support the development of her internal supervisor in her therapy work. I became aware of this model during my reading on supervision in the caring professions. I am on a journey of being able to reflect on my own practice during a supervision session while maintaining my presence with the supervisee. I have noticed occasions when the reflection in action has led to a change of direction in the moment. One example was when I reflected on whether I was following a line of questions to satisfy my own interest and curiosity rather than being in service of the client. I can evidence how reflecting in action has enhanced my practice, however, I still feel like a beginner and am looking forward to continuing to improve my ability to access my internal supervisor resource in the moment. Rickard indicated that she had observed that:

"supervisees who are naturally reflective, who have a clear sense of who they are in relation to others, find it easier to know what thoughts, feelings and emotions in the room belong to them as opposed to the client" (2011, p28).

I believe I am more competent at utilising reflection on action after coaching and supervision sessions. After each supervision session I have written a reflective note following the framework provided under the heading of supervision reflexivity later in part three. The opportunity to reflect on learnings from the session I have found essential to embed the learning and any changes in practice required as well as recognising my strengths.

One method of evidencing the change in practice is to create the space for reflection immediately after the supervision session. This ensures that you capture your evidence while it is fresh in your mind. There are many ways to do this which I have described in part two of this book. I would also encourage you to revisit your reflections a couple of weeks later and add to them where appropriate. My experience is that producing the first reflections generates further thoughts over a period of the next few days and even weeks. A record of your reflections can also be a useful prompt for bringing topics to supervision.

I concur with Rickard's view that *"self-awareness (the recognition of our thoughts, feelings, motives, desires and internal processes as they occur), and reflexivity (our ability to know our thoughts and feelings about them) would appear crucial to self-understanding and insight"* (2011, p28).

The creation of a safe space to reflect is a pre-condition for effective coaching supervision. The supervision relationship is collaborative in its nature and requires both partners to be skilled in self-reflection theory and practice in order for the coach to achieve personal growth and improve their practice. There are a number of models to support reflection in supervision, some of which I have already alluded to and which I describe in further detail in this chapter.

An inventory of a coach supervisor's reflective skill requirements

First though, I thought it would be useful to define the reflective skills required to be an effective coach supervisor. This is not an exhaustive list and I have consciously considered the skills only through the lens of reflection. I have drawn from the work of eminent authors and researchers in the field of supervision. Some have a focus on the coaching profession and others are from the caring professions who use supervision routinely in their professional practice. I have also considered the perspective of leading professional coaching associations.

Questioning and listening skills

- Ability to use various forms of questions to elicit further information
- Ability to respond to the supervisee using skills in clarifying, summarising and paraphrasing, and recognising transference and counter-transference
- The ability to be 'present' in the conversation.

Reflective skills

- The ability to recognise your own skills and the impact they can have on the supervisory interaction
- Ability to check own ideas, preconceptions and hypotheses 'in action' and amend approach when

you believe it is required in the service of the client
- The ability to evaluate (reflecting on action) the effects of your approach to supervision on the supervisee and the supervision relationship.

Observing skills

- Recognising progress and acknowledging it with the supervisee
- Noticing themes and patterns in your work with the supervisee and between the supervisee and their coaching practice.

Transparency

- Skilled in using self-disclosure appropriately
- Being fluent and open about your way(s) of working
- Being open in providing your own opinion without imposing it on the supervisee
- Being able to justify and discuss the reasons for interventions made.

Feedback

- Being able to stay with the supervisee's fears and anxieties
- Responding to the supervisee in a non-judgemental manner based on the belief that the supervisee is resourceful and is acting in the best way they can at that moment and is open to gaining new insight

- Ability to provide positive feedback authentically.

Sensitivity to wider social issues

- Being aware of the social and organisational context within which the supervisee is working with their clients and how this influences the supervision relationship
- Noticing the influence of the supervisee's social background, beliefs and values on the supervision relationship and their wider practice context.

Creativity and flexibility

- The skills to be able to create and offer a variety of different models, methods and tools for reflection.

Adapted from Rolfe's skills of reflective supervision (2013, p124-125)

Reflective challenge

Reflect critically on the list of reflective supervision skills provided and, in your role as coach supervisor, identify your strengths and areas for development. Consider how to build on your strengths and plan the next steps relating to your development areas.

Comparing and contrasting different approaches to coach supervision

There are a number of models of supervision have developed as the coaching profession has begun to mature. In my own supervision practice I have chosen to use a number of supervision models in order to compare and contrast them and to explore my effectiveness in their utilisation. These include the seven-eyed model, CLEAR model, the full spectrum model and Proctor's alliance model of supervision. I will also discuss other techniques that I have used in my coaching practice which have a relevance to supervision and reflective practice.

The seven-eyed coach supervision model

The seven-eyed supervision model was developed by Hawkins in the late 1980s and has a systems-based starting point of understanding the way human beings connect and interrelate. It is a globally recognised model in the coaching profession.

The power of the model for me is the potential for new insight and awareness to be created within a safe structure, which also looks at the relationship between coach and supervisor and the wider systems context that the coach is working in. The model is equally adept and flexible in supporting a wide range of coaches from those just starting their coaching journey through to very experienced coaches. I was particularly struck by the insights which came from the parallel process and the supervisor's self-reflection. Initially, I developed a script with potential questions to use with each eye of the model. I also endeavoured to use all seven eyes of the model in the first supervision sessions I undertook. On reflection, and in discussion with my supervisor, I can see that it was my desire to understand and be competent in the use of the model which initially drove this approach rather than the needs of the supervisee. I have now modified my approach to flow with the client and to focus in on one of the eyes based on my intuition and reflecting on what the supervisee is bringing to the session.

Analysis of my reflective logs evidenced the need with those supervisees who were relatively new to coaching to focus on the content of the coaching session they had undertaken with clients. Therefore my supervision was mostly tactical, focusing on modes 2 and 3. This focus is supported by Hawkins and Shohet who argue that "*As a general rule supervisees who are new to the work need to start with most of the supervision focusing on the content of the work with the client and the detail of what happened in the session*" (2012, p107).

I also sensed and heard evidence of the supervisees' anxiety in terms of their performance as coach. Hawkins and Shohet subscribe to the view that good supervision using the model "*must involve all seven processes although not necessarily in every session*" (2012, p106). I would argue from my own experience that this statement puts pressure on the supervisor to work across all seven modes and that this is not always in the interests of the client. I would also argue that part of the supervisor's development using this model is being able to sense intuitively which modes to use and which not to use in a session and always focusing on the presenting issue and being in service of the client.

For those of you who, like me, value a script to provide structure to your learning when using a new model I have included the script:

Seven-eyed model script template

Mode 1 Bringing the coachee into the room

- Close your eyes and see the beginning of your last session with the coachee in front of you.
- How did the session start?
- What are you seeing, sensing, feeling, what is the environment like, how is the coachee as they enter the room?
- Where do you meet the coachee?
- What do they look like?
- What is your contract with them?
- How did you become to be working with them?
- What were your first impressions of the coachee?

Mode 2 Coach interventions

- What have you done with the coachee that you haven't discussed here?

- What else would you have liked to have done?
- What is the wildest thing you could do with the client?
- Identify options and then role play chosen option from coach and coachee perspective
- What do you need to do next?

Mode 3 The relationship between the coach and coachee

- What is the relationship between you and the coachee?
- If the two of you were marooned on a desert island what would happen?
- If you were two animals what type of animal would you be?
- What might the coachee be projecting on to you the coach?
- How did you come to this conclusion about the coachee? (How do you know what you know?)
- How else might you think about this client?
- "I noticed that your voice and physiology (breathing, facial expression, tone, musculature, skin colour etc.) changed when you started to talk about this client. Can you notice what is going on in you at that time?"

Mode 4 The coach's own experience

- What buttons get pressed for you when working with the coachee?

- Does the coachee remind you of anybody?
- What did you want to say to the person the coachee reminds you of?
- Can you say this to the coachee?

Mode 5 The parallel process

- What is emanating between the supervisor and coach which could be a parallel process between the coach and coachee?
- What are you doing with me here and now that your client is doing with you?
- Is there something different happening in the room to our normal relationship?
- *What is going on for me here is ##########. Is there a relationship between what I am thinking, sensing or feeling and the situation with your client?*
  Hawkins and Shohet (2012, p101)
- Let's take a minute to look at how you and I are doing today?
- Any feelings about how we are working or relating?
- Before we stop shall we take a look at what is going on in this space between us?

Mode 6 Supervisor's own self-reflections

- For the supervisor to notice what is going on for them: Images, Thoughts, Fantasies, Feelings, Body Sensations
- Follow up with a tentative offering. A wondering out loud or noticing statement

- What is different to what I normally think and feel in this supervision relationship?

Mode 7 The wider system context

- What is the culture of the organisation the coachee is working in?
- What is going on in the sector that the coachee may bring in to the room consciously or subconsciously? e.g. banking sector
- What about the client's family and the client's profession?
- What are the organisational behaviours?
- What about gender split, nationalities?
- Is there anything in the system which may be causing the dilemma?
- Tell me about the client's background and their culture?
- What resource do they have which they are not utilising or could utilise more?
- What is the client carrying for their family or team or organisation?
- Why have they come for support now and why you?
- When and where else have they had these difficulties/ issues?

CLEAR model of supervision

The CLEAR model was developed by Hawkins in the 1980s to support supervision in the helping professions and was then adapted for coaching (Hawkins & Shohet 2006, p 61). The following is a description of the model:

C	Contract	Coaching conversations start with establishing the coachee's desired outcomes, i.e. goals, understanding what needs to be covered and agreeing any basic ground rules or roles.
L	Listen	Using active listening and catalytic interventions (see the Heron Intervention Styles) the coach develops the coachee's understanding of the situation in which s/he wants to effect a difference.
E	Explore Feelings	Having elicited a full picture of the situation the coach encourages the person to express feelings connected with the situation.
	Explore Options	Through questioning, reflection and generation of insight, coaches work with the coachee to create different options for handling the issue.
A	Action	Having explored the various dynamics within the situation and developed various options for handling it, the coachee chooses a way forward and agrees the first steps to take.
R	Review	Reviewing the actions that have been agreed completes the conversation. The coach also encourages feedback from the coachee on what was helpful about the coaching process, what was difficult and what they would like to be different in future coaching sessions (see section on feedback).

The CLEAR model offers a simple process which is excellent for building confidence for a new supervisor. It provides clarity regarding the contracting and specific outcomes which the client identifies and provides a clear steer and focus for the supervisor, particularly when a client goes off track. It can feel like a rigid linear process and a supervisor needs to be aware that, in reality, the supervisee moves forward and back through the process and acknowledging that this is OK internally is important as this understanding allows the conversation to flow. The model offers a very clear call to action. My experience is that asking supervisees to reflect on the process is sometimes difficult when they are still immersed in their own stuff. What seems to work better is an encouragement to the supervisee to make space to reflect on the session immediately after it ends and suggest that they maintain a supervision session reflective log. I now start each session with three questions aimed at eliciting the learning from the previous session. This approach is aligned with adult learning theory.

Hawkins and Shohet (2012, p239 revised to use the word YOU instead of WE)

- What did you learn that you didn't know before you came into the last supervision session and couldn't have arrived at alone?
- What new capability did you generate in the session?
- What new resolve have you acquired?

Proctor's model of supervision

Proctor (1986) defined three elements which she indicated should be used in counselling supervision; normative, formative and restorative. These elements have value in coaching supervision as well. Hay (2007) re-labelled restorative as supportive when applied to coaching to reflect the less traumatic nature of the coaching process when compared to counselling. The model was subsequently renamed the Supervision Alliance Model by Proctor.

The normative aspects of supervision relate to ensuring that the supervisee is practising in a competent and ethical way. This includes working in accordance with the the law and within whatever professional boundaries and standards apply.

The formative aspect is aimed at encouraging development and growth in the supervisee by the use of feedback, direct guidance, challenge or role modelling. The aim is to engage the supervisee in active self-awareness, development of skills and increased knowledge of theoretical models.

Finally the supportive aspect focuses on providing the supervisee with a reflective space to ensure that they are able to discuss transference or counter-transference issues. This may involve challenging the supervisee's perceptions about emotions, issues or approaches. It could also include recommending that the supervisee seeks more in-depth personal support if their own personal issues have begun to intrude into their professional practice. In addition, this aspect provides the encouragement and support to help the supervisee if they experience feelings of self-doubt or insecurity. The nature of the model encourages and supports the supervisor in the identification of the right element to focus on. However, in my opinion it does not necessarily pick up the different modes of a coaching relationship as effectively as the seven-eyed model.

The full spectrum supervision model

This model was developed by the coach supervision academy. It is a professional development tool which has a combination of traditional and contemporary methods, models and theoretical approaches. The model has at its core a focus on coaching presence. As well as using knowledge gained from considering models of supervision, it also covers body, mind and spirit. Murdoch and Arnold describe the model as "*an eclectic mix of theoretical approaches synergistically combined into a holistic systemic framework*" (2013, p.xix).

The Full Spectrum Model (FSM) benefits coaches through the opening of new fields of awareness and knowledge through consideration of the coach, the client and the system they are working in. It also recognises that coach supervision is a multi-layered activity that is most effective when it is seen as a learning partnership between two professionals. I was struck by the reference to boundary management. The model gives consideration to the need for supervisors to be open to both their humanity and to holding authority. Murdoch and Arnold (2013) argue that the FSM is aligned with Schön's theory of learning in action and learning on action and that reflective learning holds the FSM model together. To clarify this argument they indicate that reflective practice can be considered to be:

> *"…the invisible thread and the core generic competency that gives coaching supervisors the tools to help us help others learn how they learn and to then learn, unlearn and relearn as we encounter new experiences, insights and learning"* (2013, p94).

In the context of coach supervision, Murdoch and Arnold use a definition of reflective learning adapted from Amulya (2008) which states that reflective learning is:

> *"…the active process of witnessing, inquiring and exploring into our own experience(s) in order to examine that experience and to create the possibility of learning from that experience" (2013, p95).*

Murdoch and Arnold describe the model as being a 360-degree inquiry which considers all aspects of a supervisor's practice. Their view, and one I concur with, is that this process is not linear. They offer a simple set of reflective questions which I have adapted for use after a supervision session.

- What happened in the session? What did you notice and what did you miss?
- Describe what you were thinking and feeling during the session and how did you behave as a result?
- What learning are you taking from how you were as supervisor in the session?
- How do you intend to apply the learning in your future supervision practice?

Adapted from simple reflective questions (Murdoch and Arnold 2013, p103)

The model is based on the principle that, as we become more reflective as practitioners, we engage more in our own learning and understand better our own personal stories which leads us to be more authentic. This has benefits in both our professional practice and more generally in our lives.

I have lived by this principle over the last decade. In my life in general it has supported me in being more authentic and also in facing up to some of the traits and beliefs I had which I disliked and were no longer serving me positively. I have challenged myself to consider these traits in depth and make changes. At some points I have felt the need for some additional support including psychodynamic therapy sessions.

Some of the areas I worked on included my relationship with money, a focus on self to the detriment of others, being careful and not taking risks and my perspective on winning and achieving.

My experience evidences that this is a deeply courageous, difficult yet potentially transformational process. Murdoch and Arnold confirm this by stating that *"Central here is that learning and change is an emotional, social and psychological process that must be handled, honoured and respected with care, courage, clarity and compassion"* (2013, p113).

The relevance of the NLP communication model

A supervisor's knowledge of the NLP communication model[4] supports the development of understanding how external events can, through a client's map of the world impact on their state and physiology that translates into behaviour which impacts on results. This relates to the presupposition that you can't not communicate. Through our representational systems we are communicating all the time. It is important for coaches to understand the impact they have on others. It is also important that a supervisor is aware of their own map of the world and that they assess whether what they are sensing is their own stuff or whether it relates to a parallel process, transference or counter-transference.

---

4 The NLP Communication Model describes how you make sense of your world and the behaviours that you manifest as a result

Supervision reflexivity

I developed a template to support my reflections following research on reflexivity which I now use in my coach supervision practice. You will see reference to my research in the template as I indicate where the questions come from should you wish to read more on the topic of reflexivity.

Initially, I asked the supervisee the first three questions at the end of the session. My experience was that the supervisee was still immersed in their own thinking at that moment and subsequently I modified my approach to ask the questions at the beginning of the following session. This is an improvement but still isn't perfect as some supervisees are methodical about creating space after the session to reflect and others are more inconsistent in their reflective focus. On balance, I think it is appropriate to model the expectation that both supervisor and supervisee plan in some reflective time independently immediately after each session and that the questions are answered by the supervisee during this time and then reported back at the following session. These questions help in pinning down the new insight and awareness gained and act as a call to action for the supervisee.

I find the challenge/disturb me questions to be a great way of testing out how brave and courageous I had been in the session. Had I named what had challenged or disturbed me? Similarly, answering what question was my heart, asking me to articulate, picks up on the emotions I was feeling in the session and checks out whether I named them appropriately and in service of the supervisee. These questions also check out whether there was any transference or counter-transference going on that I had not picked up in the session.

Over time I have found the scoring approach in the last section of the template to be less meaningful. It does not necessarily support deeper reflection, although it has provided me with a tool to track patterns and my overall progress.

I hope it is helpful for you to see a populated version of the template to give a sense of how I use it to support my own reflection and obtain feedback from my supervisee.

Reflexivity note template

Mark Bisson Coaching supervision session reflexivity template.

Name of coach GJ   Date 15/6/15

Supervisee's reflections on last session

Hawkins and Shohet (2012, p239 wording revised including using the word YOU instead of WE).

1. What have you learnt that you didn't know before you came into the last supervision session and couldn't have arrived at alone?

- How much I was making assumptions on behalf of the coachee and to focus on holding back and give the coachee the space to lead.
- If I was in a similar situation again I would have held back a bit more. The approach I took did avert a potential constructive dismissal case.

2. What new capability, insight or awareness did you generate either during the session or during further reflection after the session?

- The session raised my awareness around not having to take responsibility and in subsequent coaching sessions I have felt more relaxed in the knowledge that I do not have to take responsibility.
- Having self-awareness during coaching sessions about my past regarding my need to take responsibility and consciously deciding not to bring that into the session.
- I learnt that the confidential nature of supervision and the safe space created is of value. I could not have talked to anyone else about the case. I need to be careful about what I reveal in my own coaching sessions.

3. What new resolve have you acquired?

- To reflect on what was going on for me during

the session and learn from that in terms of what I would do differently regarding the use of my inner self.

- To try and have the same rapport without getting so attached while still having a deep connection with the client which is authentically me.

Reflexivity

What impact/influence did I have as coach supervisor during the session?

- Having been sick for a week I think my low energy impacted the session negatively although I think this was due to a mindset going into the session that I would not perform at my best. However, at the beginning of the session G shared that she was not feeling well due to a sinus infection and I then shared how I was feeling in terms of the virus I had. This had the impact of taking away my anxiety regarding performing at my best and I relaxed more and became more present.
- I did re-read my notes from the previous session to remind myself of the supervision topic to support my preparation. I was able to reflect back the topic to G when she could not remember initially what she had discussed.

"Building rapport by putting some of myself as interviewer into the session, possibly by raising similar or different experiences (Arksey and Knight" (1999 p139).

Did I do this in the session and if so what was the impact from my perspective as coach supervisor?

- I talked to G about her recent skiing holiday to Austria which I recalled from the notes of the previous session.
- Where did I improvise and what was the impact?
- I felt I was challenging in my questions to G regarding any potential collusion in her relationship with the coachee. I used mode 1 of the seven-eyed model as my sense was that how she felt and what she thought of her client was key to G being able to create awareness of how appropriate or not her chosen approach with the client had been.
- I asked what buttons get pressed for her when working with the client. This prompted one reflection that at first she felt less adequate in terms of could she do what he required from a coach. The third session had required her to be brave/courageous and as a result it felt like a more balanced relationship and she had received an email the following day from him saying that it had given him lots to work on/reflect on.
- This also led to a question I asked about parallel process and G reflected on the empathy and frustration she shared with regard to her own perceived inadequacies as an MD.

Were there any other reflections in terms of how I conducted the session?

- G said I had gauged the space well in terms of giving her time to think and work from a coaching position with her. I was challenged by this as with my other supervisees it is far more balanced in the session in terms of me providing guidance and feedback and I described the difference with G who I perceive as more experienced than I am and this impacted subconsciously the amount of feedback or advice I provided and that I had a feeling of anxiety which was not present with my other supervisees. This was a real breakthrough for me as I felt G valued the feedback and advice I then provided and supported the internal perception of my growth as a supervisor and that I had received permission by G to be in an equal relationship with her.

- I also shared that the topics with other supervisees tended to be more tactical around the use of models, contracting etc. and I was seen by them as the experienced expert coach. The fact that G brought difficult/stretching topics to our sessions made me feel respected for the value I added as a supervisor.

- I also reflected that I am now using elements of CLEAR, full spectrum and seven-eyed models interchangeably in the moment with some reference to my notes which is easier to do when delivering on Skype.

In the next session I need to be more specific in asking G what she needs from me as her supervisor so the joint contract for the session is clear.

What did I pick up in terms of the supervisee's body language or from their voice?

- Familiarity with G's eye cues and moving about in her chair when she is thinking.

What is the one thing from the session which challenged me or disturbed me?

• I was challenged by G's request for feedback and advice.

What is the one emotion which this supervisee creates in me?

• Warmth and respect for her coaching ability and the tough job she has leading her business. A desire to nurture and support. I think this is within my professional boundaries and picks up on my value of wanting to support people to learn and grow.

Notes to take during interview Easterby-Smith
(2002, p123)

1.What was the relationship like between coach supervisor and supervisee?

Closed									Open
1	2	3	4	5	6	7	8	9	10

Evidence of the challenging topics G brings to supervision and our discussion at the end of the session with regard to G's desire to ask for my perspective and advice. Also G talked about three family bereavements since we last spoke.

2. What was the attitude of the supervisee?

Disengaged									Engaged
1	2	3	4	5	6	7	8	9	10

When we got into the session G was very engaged, however, how she was feeling in terms of her health did have an impact.

3. What is my level of confidence as coach supervisor?

Unconfident									Very confident
1	2	3	4	5	6	7	8	9	10

G's request for advice did give me a boost in terms of external validation of my credibility as supervisor.

Focusing on bringing 'learning in action' (Schön 1983) into my consciousness, what new meaning or learning did I take from my inner self during the coaching session?

It's OK to be the expert when it is used appropriately and is not about ego and power is what I was sensing in the moment. The use of expert comes from a heart place of wanting to support someone in their growth and development. I am not thinking this is Mark Bisson MA although that is of course what my qualifications say I am. It is not a badge I use (reflecting on my conversation with S about SW and her different states of being).

My confidence in my supervision practice is growing and continuing to read on the topic helps my confidence in that I have valuable knowledge to impart which I can do with credibility. To do so for me requires strong images for me to hold on to such as the dance floor and balcony example (Schön 1983).

I have also used a similarly structured template to record my reflections on my own supervision sessions. I have provided a populated example to provide you with some content on my own reflective journey as a coach supervisor.

As topics or patterns come into my awareness I maintain a log to consider bringing to supervision. I have since learnt the importance of not just logging the topic but reflecting on it before the supervision session so that I have developed thought and reflections rather than working this in the moment of the supervision session. This enables a better flow to the conversation and I am more open to feedback, advice and guidance. The section on previous actions holds me to account for my learning and growth and is a record of my progress. I find this of value in reflecting on my journey. The sections on learnings and next steps provide a light structure for my reflective writing without being constraining. I often use one of the models of reflection contained in this book as the framework for my reflection and then record the learnings in the template log. I really like the next steps approach to action planning which is particularly helpful for recording milestone steps along the way to a longer-term goal. For me the milestones help me to stay on track.

Example of reflexivity template used in my own supervision

SV Supervision note   12/3/14
Introduction to the session

I introduced the session by providing an update on the actions I had undertaken as a result of the last supervision with S. I also discussed my sense of how my supervision practice had developed since we last spoke.

What did I bring to the session?

Do I want to cover the critical parent/adaptive child issue with G? I would like to discuss this with S at my next supervision session. There is something that I hold from my childhood in this respect. On both occasions I have requested feedback she has started with a negative. However, my belief is that the comments have validity. Is this me being adaptive? I have an issue about taking feedback as criticism.

First session that I have worked totally intuitively. It felt good although I did pick up the transference/counter-transference which I think I will bring to supervision.

I definitely described some of my experiences as a coach. I also shared that the lower part of J's face reminded me of my brother and occasionally I had to catch myself as I saw my brother. I did also say that there were no issues of transference for me. This was something I had an awareness of and was able to manage any emotions which came up as a result of the internal comparison I was making visually. J then shared an example from his coaching experience where he was coaching the son of an old boss.

Evidence of my growing confidence as supervisor and in my coaching practice

A manager at EBC who has a number of areas to be coached on relating to a self-identified development plan based on reflections from a 360 and Facet 5 report and who has asked to be coached on how to be a coach as well. Modelling behaviours and approaches, training in the session by referencing where I am with a certain model e.g. GROW. Whilst in the coaching moment, I have reflected on my development and my ability to parallel run this request within the sessions. I am enjoying the stretch and I am also wondering if this is playing in a desire for me to be seen as 'the Expert'.

H session 2

This session was a significant breakthrough in my supervision practice. I believe I flowed with H and used elements of the seven-eyed model without following the script rigidly. I asked insightful questions and following Proctor's model (Management, Educational, Supportive). I acted as a role model and flowed between the three functions. I provided space for H to reflect and explore. I also provided feedback and specific encouragement regarding the techniques and skills she had used in her coaching practice. I helped H identify transference which had occurred between her and her coachee. I named what I was sensing and feeling about the duration of the coach supervision session and how my feelings were similar to and different from H's feelings about ending the coaching session.

I felt really uplifted about being able to support H to remove the burden and the pressure she had been feeling.

Actions from previous session

With the client in ES I can see that I have a duty of care to the organisation who have commissioned me as well as my client. I need to have a conversation with the Director asking what she thinks is going on here? And describe what I am sensing. Which is that the situation is untenable, do a deal, pay off.

I had this conversation and a compromise route is now in progress and the assistant director is looking to use me as a coach with another senior manager.

Think about the question "Do I attract clients who are similar or different to me and what does that say about me?"

Three of my supervisees are very driven, motivated, positive people who are achievement focused which is similar to how I perceive myself.

However, there is only one supervisee who is feelings led as I perceive myself to be.

When I assess my coaching relationships that I have currently, I have clients who lack self-confidence which is not as I perceive myself or the view of others I have sought feedback from. Other coaches have a real integrity and live by their personal values and I believe this is similar to me.

I should wait until the following session to ask the supervisee for feedback on the previous session. This gives them an opportunity to reflect. At the end of the session they are in their own stuff and not really in a place to provide feedback effectively. Also to notice what type of feedback is being provided; is it constructive, developmental or destructive?

I listened to the above advice and now ask supervisees to reflect on the session and then I ask for feedback at the beginning of the next session using a set of questions I have developed from reading Hawkins and Shohet (2012, 239).

The questions are:

- What have we learnt that neither of us knew before we came into supervision?
- What have we learnt that neither of us could have arrived at alone?
- What new capability have we generated in this session?
- What new resolve have we each acquired?

What did I learn from this session?

We discussed the use of the Hawkins and Shohet questions and what the wording of the questions could do for a supervisee at the beginning of their coaching journey, and the appropriateness of the supervisor sharing learnings and whether the supervisee would be able to recognise what WE had learnt. I reflected back that G, an experienced coach, had also struggled with the wording of the questions. My reflection was that they would struggle to do this. I have therefore decided to modify the questions to focus on them by using YOU instead of WE.

We also discussed asking G about her intent in providing me with feedback. We delved into my childhood at school and at home in terms of my focus on feedback being negative rather than developmental. S talked about peers of our generation having similar reports at school, about 'could do better' and my reflections on my lack of maturity at school and not being able to find something I was passionate about or had an intrinsic motivation around which I now have.

S challenged me to reframe my position by referring to feedback being a gift and to put the 'critical parent' issue on the bridge until the moment was right to include it in a supervision conversation. I do see that viewing feedback as a gift is a significant change of mindset which would have a positive impact on many aspects of my life. As I am not a gifts person I may prefer to see it as a 'caring touch'.

We discussed the parallel process which had run with two supervisees. With HH I need to check in where she is at with regard to contracting and knowing when to refer a client. I also gained insight that, in offering to extend our supervision session, I was rescuing her and that this could lead to building a dependency and that the rescuing could be driven by my desire to be seen as the expert. I think this is about evidencing my skills which in turn leads to me being more confident as supervisor. I am not sure what this means for my practice as supervisor, as part of the role of supervisor is to be the expert. Hawthorne (1975) discusses how to find an appropriate way of taking authority and handling the power of the supervisor's role. Hawthorne recognises that this is both difficult and crucial. Stoltenberg and Delworth (1987) suggest a model for identifying a supervisor's development. I believe I am now at level 2 where *"The supervisor now sees that the process of supervision is more complex and multi-dimensional than he or she had imagined."* (Hawkins and Shohet 2012, p81).

In discussing the coaching relationship with JC, S suggested that combining working an issue with training on coaching could mean that both of us were not as present as we could be as we may both be 'in our heads' rather than being present with regard to our Head, Heart and Gut. S suggested that I propose that we use the final part of our sessions to focus on reflection on process, theories and models used. This should enable the first part of the session to be more effective.

I asked for feedback on my practice, given that in my first session with S she had said that I needed to go deeper and that I was being too broad in an attempt to cover everything. S said that she saw evidence that I was being more reflective but that I was not working through and resolving the issues I identified but instead I was saving them up for my supervision with S, which is absolutely accurate. In terms of my development I need to go one step further and begin to identify solutions myself as part of my reflective process.

To support me in this S suggested two further questions which I could add to my reflexivity template.

1. What is the one emotion which this client creates in me?
2. What is the one thing from the session that challenged me or disturbed me?

Finally, I indicated that when asked about the difference between transference and counter-transference I could not articulate an answer although I had read on the topic. I asked S for her definition:

Transference = one-way street

Supervisor picks up something from the client

Counter-Transference = two-way street

Either supervisee or supervisor pick up something from the other person, make a judgement using their own map of the world and then project it back on the other person.

Reflections since the session

Next Steps:

*   Refresh my understanding of the full spectrum model from my course notes/internet.
*   Alter the Hawkins and Shohet questions to 'you' rather than 'we'
*   Put critical parent insight on the bridge until I feel the moment is right with G.
*   Plan the last third of the coaching sessions with J to

be training in how to coach to provide the space for the coaching in the first part of the session to be the best it can be.

- Pick up one nugget from each supervision session. Ask myself what is the one thing from the session that challenged me or disturbed me.
- Add questions to self-reflective template. What is the one emotion which this client creates in me?
- To see feedback as a caring touch.
- Check out with H what her contract is with the client she discussed in our session and knowing when to refer.
- Work at being more tuned in to moments when counter-transference takes place and naming it in supervision sessions.

Reflective challenge

Think about your approach to reviewing coaching and supervision relationships and whether you adopt a consistent approach to obtaining feedback when you reach the end of a relationship. What action do you need to take as a result of your reflection?

PART FOUR

Your future journey

"It is not sufficient simply to have an experience in order to learn. Without reflecting upon this experience it may quickly be forgotten, or its learning potential lost. It is from the feelings and thoughts emerging from this reflection that generalisations or concepts can be generated. And it is generalisations that allow new situations to be tackled effectively."
(Gibbs 1988, p9)

Your future journey in using self-reflection in your practice

I hope you have enjoyed the experience of reading this book and have found it informative, supportive and challenging. Now I would like to offer you a moment to consider the thoughts and feelings that have emerged for you from your reflections on its content and the reflective challenges you have undertaken so that you ensure that your learning potential is captured.

What you consider to be excellence in your practice now will be different in a year's time. This reflects my awareness that the more you learn the more you know there is to learn. When I attended a module of my Masters titled 'higher professional coaching skills' we undertook an exercise with a partner on the first day. We used the ICF core competencies to check where we were on our journey. I recall consistently marking myself around seven out of ten. We then undertook ten days of intensive experiential learning and at the end of the programme we repeated the competency assessment. My self-assessment was then fives and sixes across the competencies. The significant amount of new insight and awareness had brought me to a place of humility regarding my competence. I realised that before the programme I had been over-confident regarding my ability and experience as a coach and my new knowledge had helped me understand that I had been just scratching the surface.

Reflective challenge

Think about what you have learnt about yourself and your practice through reflecting on it during the course of reading this book. How certain can you be of its accuracy or truthfulness? Do you trust the results of your reflections more or less than you trust the knowledge you obtain from professional journals and research papers? What is the reason for that? Adapted from Rolfe (2011, p25)

Now think about your experience of reading this book:

- What have you learnt about yourself regarding self-reflection in your practice?
- What thoughts and feelings have surfaced?
- What are you good at?
- What do you need to do more or less of?
- What new awareness or insight do you have that you couldn't have arrived at without reading this book?
- Which part of the book did you enjoy most and what are the reasons?
- Which part of the book did you find the most challenging and what were the reasons that it was challenging?
- What is your greatest fear regarding using self-reflection in your practice?
- What question is your heart asking you to ask yourself about your self-reflection journey going forward?

Now I would encourage you to write an end of book report about yourself that highlights what you are good at and your development areas. You could use the ICF or another recognised professional association's core competencies to rate yourself. Include in your narrative the reasons for your scores.

- What are your beliefs about self-reflection?
- What are your priority areas for development and what informed your conclusion?
- What patterns or themes have you identified in respect of the topics and issues your clients bring to coaching and supervision?
- What patterns or themes of issues have I taken to supervision?
- What issues do I not take to supervision?

Looking to the future

- Having answered these questions, what do you want to do next in your journey of becoming a more self-reflective coach or supervisor?
- How is this representative of the self-reflective practitioner that you want to be?
- Thinking about your learning journey ahead, what are the milestones you are aiming at and what are the next steps you can take to start your journey?

- How will you know when you have achieved your goals?
- What will be the impact on your clients and those you supervise?

Conclusion

I would like to acknowledge all of the eminent authors and researchers working in the field of self-reflection, particularly those working in healthcare, education and social work and of course, coaching, who have impacted my approach as a practitioner. If you are interested in specific areas of research I would encourage you to read further using the reference list that follows.

There is still much to do in terms of researching the impact of self-reflection in the coaching profession with regard to evidencing the quality of our practice and the positive impact which results for those we coach and supervise. As a profession I think we have been through our formative and slightly rebellious teenage years and are now moving on to our 'young adult' stage. For me, this means we are open to new learning and are pushing the boundaries in terms of our skills and abilities. But there is still so much more we know we need to learn.

This should mean that the coaching profession is in a place of humility regarding the need and purpose of self-reflection. How self-reflection can support us both individually and as a profession in our lifelong journey of knowing ourselves in the service of our clients is an awareness which I hope this book has created in you.

"Self-reflection is a humbling process which has no destination. It is driven by an intrinsic motivation to know ourselves so that we can be the best that we can be" (Bisson 2016).

I would be really interested in hearing about personal stories from your journey of self-reflection so please do get in touch with me via my website www.risecoachingandmentoring.com.

References

Amas, D. (2007). We all love playing in the sand! Using sand play therapy in critical reflection with students in practice placement. *Journal of Practice Teaching & Learning* 7(2) 2006-07, pp.6-24. © 2007 Whiting & Birch Ltd

Amulya, Joy (2008). What is reflective practice? *Center for Reflective Community Practice.* Massachusetts Institute of Technology
accessed [online] http://www.bing.com/ search?q=amulya+what+is+reflective+practice& form=IE11TR&src=IE11TR&pc=HPNTDFJS on 20th April 2016

Anderson, A., Knowles, Z., and Gilbourne, D. (2004). Reflective practice for sports psychologists: Concepts, models, practical implications, and thoughts on dissemination. *Sport Psychologist, 18*. pp.188-201

Arksey, Hilary and Knight, Peter (1999) *Interviewing for Social Scientists*. London: Sage.

Arnheim, Rudolf (1969). *Visual Thinking*. Berkeley. University of California Press.

Atkins, S. and Murphy, K. (1994).'Reflective practice'. *Nursing standard* 8(39)

Bachkirova, E., Cox, T. and Clutterbuck, D. (2014). *The Complete Handbook of Coaching*. London. Sage.

Bain, J. D., Ballantyne, R., Packer, J. and Mills, C. (1999). Using journal writing to enhance student teachers' reflectivity during field experience placements.

[Article]. *Teachers & Teaching, 5*, 51.

Black, P. E. and Plowright, D. (2010). A multi-dimensional model of reflective learning for professional development. *Reflective Practice, 11*(2), pp. 245-258. doi:10.1080/14623941003665810

Bluckert, P. (2004). 'Improving professional practice – the role of supervision in coaching', from www.pbcoaching.com.

Bolton, G. (2010) *Reflective Practice, Writing and Professional Development* (3rd edition), California; SAGE publications.

Bond, M. and Holland, S. (1998). *Skills of Clinical Supervision for Nurses*. Buckingham, University Press.

Borton, T. (1970), *Reach, Touch and Teach*. London: Hutchinson.

Boud, David. Keogh, Rosemary and Walker, David. (1985). *Reflection: turning experience into learning*. New York. Nichols publishing company.

Boyd, E. and Fales, A. (1983). 'Reflective learning: The Key to Learning from Experience'. *Journal of Humanistic Psychology, 23*(2).

Branch, William and Paranjape, Anuradha (2002). FEEDBACK AND REFLECTION: TEACHING METHODS FOR CLINICAL SETTINGS. *Academic Medicine*: December 2002 – Volume 77 – Issue 12, Part 1 – pp. 1185-1188 Accessed [online] at http://journals.lww.com/academicmedicine/pages/articleviewer.aspx?year=2002&issue=12000&article=00005&type=fulltext on 29 March 2016.

Brookfield, S. (2009). The concept of critical reflection: promises and contradictions. *European Journal of*

Social Work, 12(3), pp.293-304.

Brown, K. W. and Ryan R. M. (2003). The benefits of being present: mindfulness and its role in psychological wellbeing. *Journal of personality and social psychology*. 84(4): pp.822-848

Bugental, J.F.T. (1987), *The Art of the Psychotherapist.* New York: Norton.

Carper, B. (1978). Fundamental Patterns of Knowing in Nursing. *Advances in Nursing Science* Volume 1-Issue1-pp.13-24

Casement, P. (1985). *On learning from the patient.* London. Tavistock.

Chapman-Clarke, M. (2015). Nine words to reach zero. *Coaching at work* Vol 10 issue 6 pp.48-50

Chartered Institute for Personnel and Development. *Coach supervision, maximising the potential of coaching.* Accessed on 7/10/15 at www.cipd.co.uk/.../0/coachsuperv.pdf ·

Clark, M., and Wilson, A. (1991). Context and rationality in Mezirow's theory of transformational learning. *Adult Education Quarterly*, 41(2), pp.75-91.

Cranton, P. *Understanding and Promoting Transformative Learning: A Guide for Educators of Adults.* San Francisco: Jossey-Bass.

Cranton, P. (1996) *Professional development as transformative learning.* San Francisco:

Crawley, J. (2005) *In at the Deep End – a survival guide for teachers in Post Compulsory Education.* London: David Fulton.

Davies, Samantha (January 2012). "Embracing reflective practice". *Education for Primary Care* 23 (1): 9–12. *PMID 22306139*

De Domenico, G. (1995). Sand Tray-World Play / a comprehensive guide to the use of the sand tray in psychotherapeutic and transformational settings. Oakland, Ca: Vision Quest Images (accessed at http://vision-quest.us/VQISR/Sandtray-Worldplay_ The%20Tool_.pdf)

Dewey, John. (1933). *How We Think: A Restatement of the Relation of Reflective Thinking to The Educative Process. Boston.* Houghton Mifflin.

Downey, M. (1999) *Effective Coaching*, London: Orion Business Books.

Easterby-Smith, M., Thorpe, R. and Lowe, A. (2002). *Management Research: An introduction.* London, SAGE publications.

Ertmer, P. A., and Newby T. J. (1996). The expert learner: Strategic, self-regulated, and reflective. *Instructional Science 24*, pp.1-14

Fielding, M. (1994). Valuing difference in teachers and learners: building on Kolb's learning styles to develop a language of teaching and learning. *The Curriculum Journal* 5(3): pp.393-417

Flaherty, J. (1999). *Coaching: Evoking excellence in others.* Butterworth-Heinemann. Woburn:

Fook, J. (2006). *Beyond reflective practice: reworking the "critical" in critical reflection.* Presented at the meeting of the Professional Lifelong Learning: Beyond Reflective Practice, Leeds.

Fornreris and Campbell, *Critical Thinking and Clinical Reasoning in the Health Sciences*, Facione and Facione (eds.), California Academic Press. 6 Accessed online at http://www.insightassessment.com/content/

download/4103/42138/file/Reflective+Storytelling +as+Context+for+Critical+Thinking.pdf on 20th June 2016

Francis, D. (1995). The reflective journal: A window to preservice teachers' practical knowledge. *Teaching and Teacher Education, 11*(3), pp. 229-241.

Freire, P. (1972). *Pedagogy of the Oppressed*, London: Penguin.

Furman, Rich, Coyne, Ann and Negi Nalini Junko (2008). An International Experience for Social Work students: Self-reflection through poetry and journal writing exercises. *Journal of Teaching in Social Work*, Volume 28, Issue 1-2 pp. 71-85

Ghaye, T., and Ghaye, K. (1998). *Teaching and learning through critical reflective practice*. London: D. Fulton Publishers.

Gibbs, G. (1988) *Learning by doing: A guide to teaching and learning methods*, Oxford Centre for Staff and Learning Development, Oxford Polytechnic. London: Further Education Unit.

Graham-Pole, J. (2000). *Illness and the art of creative expression*. Oakland, CA: New Harbinger.

Gray, D. E. (2007). Facilitating management learning: Developing critical reflection through reflective tools. *Management Learning, 38*(5), pp.495-517.

Gunaratana, B.H. (2002). *Mindfulness in plain English*. Somerville, MA: Wisdom Publications

Hadot, P. (1998). The Inner Citadel – The meditations of Marcus Aurelis, London: Harvard University Press.

Harvey, M., Coulson, D., Mackaway, J. and Winchester-Seeto, T. (2010). Aligning reflection in the cooperative education curriculum. Macquarie University ResearchOnline. *Asia-Pacific Journal of Cooperative Education, 11*(3), pp.137-152.

Hatton, N. and Smith, D. (1994, July 3-6, 1994)). *Facilitating Reflection: Issues and Research.* Presented at the meeting of the Conference of the Australian Teacher Education Association (24th), Brisbane, Queensland, Australia.

Hawkins, P. and Smith, N. (2013).*Coaching, Mentoring and Organisational Consultancy: Supervision and Development.* New York. Open University Press.

Hawkins, P. and Schwenk, G. (2006). Maximising the potential of coaching, CIPD

Hawkins, P. and Shohet, R. (2012). *Supervision in the helping professions*, Maidenhead: Open University Press.

Hawthorne, L. (1975). 'Games Supervisors Play'. *Social Work* 20,3, pp.179-183

Hay, J. (2007). *Reflective Practice and Supervision for Coaches.* Maidenhead. Open University Press.

Hellison, Donald. and Templin, T. (1991). *A Reflective Approach to Teaching Physical Education.* Champaign IL: Human Kinetics.

Hillier, Yvonne (2002). Reflective Teaching on Further and Adult Education (Continuum studies in lifelong learning). Continuum International Publishing Group Ltd.

Holm, D. and Stephenson, S. (1994). *Reflection – A student's perspective.* Palmer: Burns and Bulman.

Hoogeboom, Marjolein (2011). *The Origins of Self-Reflection – How to enhance professional development among coaching psychologists* [online] accessed on 18 March 2016 at http://www.innovatiefinwerk.nl/ sites/innovatiefinwerk.nl/files/field/bijlage/m-these. hoogeboom.pdf

Huber, C. (1995). *The Fear Book*. California: Keep it Simple Books.

Inglese, Terry and Rigotti, Francesca (2011). *Students' Metaphors for Defining Their Learning Experience with Audio-Visible versus Invisible Authors. Results from a Case Study in a Social Science Discipline.* Creative Education 2011. Vol.2, No.3, 181-188 Copyright © 2011 SciRes. DOI:10.4236/ce.2011.23025

Jarvis, P. (2010). *Adult Education and Lifelong Learning: Theory and Practice* (4th ed.). New York: Routledge.

Johns, Christopher (August 1995). "Framing learning through reflection within Carper's fundamental ways of knowing in nursing". *Journal of Advanced Nursing 22 (2): 226–234. doi:10.1046/j.1365-2648.1995.22020226.x. PMID 7593941*

Johns, C. (2006). *Engaging reflection in practice: a narrative approach.* Oxford. Blackwell Publishing.

Johns, C (2004). *Becoming a Reflective Practitioner.* Blackwell Publishing.

Johns, C (2013). *Becoming a Reflective Practitioner.* Oxford. Blackwell Publishing.

Jones, R and Jones, G. (1996). *Earth Dance Drum.* Commune-E-Key. Utah:

Jung, K. (1964). *Man and his symbols.* London. Aldus Books Ltd.

Kabat-Zinn, J. (1990). *Full catastrophe living. How to cope with stress, pain and illness using mindfulness meditation.*

London: Piatkus.

Kadushin, A. (1992). *Supervision in social work*. New York: Columbia University Press

Kant, I., Guyer, P. and Wood, A. (1999). *Critique of Pure Reason*. Cambridge: Cambridge University Press.

Kirkpatrick, MK. Ford, S. and Costelloe, BP. (1997). Storytelling: an approach to client-centred care, *Nurse Educator*, 22 (2), pp.38-40

Klug, Ron (2002). *How to Keep a Spiritual Journal. A guide to journal keeping for inner growth and personal discovery* (rev. edn.), Minneapolis: Augsburg

Knowles, Malcolm. (1980). *The Modern Practice of Adult Education*. New Jersey: Cambridge Adult Education.

Kolb, D. A. (1984). *Experiential learning: Experience as the source of learning and development* (Vol. 1). Englewood Cliffs, New Jersey. Prentice-Hall.

Korsgaard, C. (2004). Fellow Creatures: Kantian Ethics and our Duties to Animals. University of Michigan lecture paper accessed online at http://scholar.google.co.uk/citations?user=6xFe8rAAAAAJ&hl=en&oi=sra on 14/6/16.

Labov; W. (1972). The transformation of experience in narrative syntax. In, Labov, W. *Language in the Inner City: Studies in the Black English Vernacular*. Philadelphia, University of Pennsylvania Press.

Lawley, J. and Tompkins, P., (2000). *Metaphors in Mind: Transformation Through Symbolic Modelling.* London: Developing Company Press.

Lawley, James and Tompkins Penny (2006). The *Cutting Edge Coaching Techniques Handbook, CIPD, Coaching at work Accessed online at http://www.cleanlanguage.co.uk/*

articles/articles/127/1/Coaching-with-Metaphor/Page1. html on 15 June 2016.

Leijen, A., Valtna, K., Leijen, D. A. J. and Pedaste, M. (2011). How to determine the quality of students' reflections? *Studies in Higher Education*, 1-15. doi:10.1 080/03075079.2010.504814

MacCormac, E. (1990). *A Cognitive Theory of Metaphor.* Cambridge, MA: MIT Press.

Macpherson, M. https://www.questia.com/magazine /1G1-214895266/critical-self-reflection-a-primer-for-leadership [online] Accessed on 17 March 2016.

McAdams, D.P. (2008). Personal narratives and the life story, in OP John, RW Robins and LA Pervin (eds), *Handbook of personality: theory and research* (3rd edition), New York: Guilford Press.

McDrury, J. and Alterio, M. (2003). Learning through storytelling in higher education: using reflection and experience to improve learning. London: Kogan Page.

McLeod, S. A. (2013). Kolb – Learning Styles. Retrieved from www.simplypsychology.org/learning-kolb.html

Mezirow, J. (1991a). *Transformative dimensions of adult learning.* San Francisco: Jossey-Bass.

Mezirow, J. (1991b). Transformation theory and cultural context: A Reply to Clarke and Wilson. *Adult Education Quarterly*, 41(3), pp.188-192.

Mezirow, J. (1995). "Transformative Theory of Adult Learning." In M. Welton (ed.), *In Defense of the Lifeworld.* Albany: State University of New York Press.

Mezirow, J. "Contemporary Paradigms of Learning."

Adult Education Quarterly, 1996, *46* (3), pp.158–172.

Mezirow, J. (1997). Transformative Learning: Theory to Practice. *New Directions for Adult and Continuing Education,* 74, pp.5–12.

Mezirow, J. (2003). Transformative learning as discourse. *Journal of Transformative Education,*1(1), pp. 58-63.

Miller, George. (1956). The Magical Number Seven plus or minus two: Some Limits on our Capacity for Processing Information. Harvard University first published in *Psychological Review*, *63*, 81-97.

Montagu, Jemima (2002). The Surrealists: Revolutionaries in art & writing 1919–1935, London: Tate Publications.

Murdoch, E. and Arnold, J. (2013). *Full Spectrum Supervision*, St Albans: Panoma Press Ltd.

O'Broin, A. and Palmer, S. (2009). Co-creating an optimal coaching alliance: A Cognitive Behavioural Coaching Perspective. *International Coaching Psychology Review*, 4(2), pp.184-194.

Ortony, A. (1993). *Metaphor and Thought*. Cambridge: Cambridge University Press.

Passmore, J. and Marianetti, O. (2013). The role of mindfulness in coaching. *The Coaching Psychologist.* 3(3), 131-138.

Paterson, Colin; Chapman, Judith (August 2013). "Enhancing skills of critical reflection to evidence learning in professional practice" (PDF). Physical Therapy in Sport 14 (3): pp.133–138. doi:10.1016/j.ptsp.2013.03.004. PMID 23643448.

Plummer, Ken (2001). *Documents of Life 2. An invitation to a critical humanism*, London: Sage.

Popper, Karl. (2002). *The Logic of Scientific Discovery*.

London: Routledge.

Proctor, B. (1986). *Supervision: a cooperative exercise in accountability in A. Marken and M. Payne (eds) Enabling and Ensuring: Supervision in practice*. Leicester National Youth Bureau/Council for education and Training in Youth and Community. Work Leicester, U.K.

Resnick, R.F. and Estrup, L. (2000). Supervision: A Collaborative Endeavour. *Gestalt Review*, 4(2): pp.121–137.

Rickard, A. (2011). The internal supervisor, Retrieved 6th October 2015 from http://www.therapytoday.net/article/show/2262/the-internal-supervisor/

Robotham, D. (1999). *The application of learning style theory in higher education teaching*. Unpublished article; available from author at Wolverhampton Business School, Compton Road West, Wolverhampton, WV3 9DX.

Rolfe, G., Freshwater, D. and Jasper, M. (2001). *Critical Reflection in Nursing and the Helping Professions: a User's Guide*. Basingstoke: Palgrave Macmillan.

Rolfe, G. and Gardner, L.D. (2006). "Do not ask who I am ..." Confession, Emancipation and (Self) Management Through Reflection. *Journal of Nursing Management*. 14 (8); pp.593-606.

Rolfe, G., Freshwater, D. and Jasper, M. (2011). *Critical reflection in practice* (2nd ed.). Houndmills, Basingstoke, Hampshire; New York: Palgrave.

Rosinski, P. (2003). *Coaching across cultures*. London: Nicholas Brealey.

Rowling, J. K. (2000).*The Goblet of Fire*. London. Bloomsbury.

Schön, Donald A. (1983). *The reflective practitioner: how professionals think in action.* New York. Basic Books.

Shapiro, J., Kasman, D. and Shafer, A. (2006). Words and Wards: A model of Reflective Writing and its Uses in Medical Education. *Journal of Medical Humanities*, 27.

Shohet, R. (2008). Passionate Supervision. London: Jessica Kingsley Publishers.

Silsbee, Doug (2008). *Presence-Based Coaching.* San Francisco. Jossey-Bass.

Smith, Mark (1999, 2006, 2013), 'Keeping a learning journal. A guide for educators and social practitioners', *the encyclopedia of informal education.* [http://infed. org/mobi/writing-and-keeping-journals-a-guide-for-educators-and-social-practitioners/. Retrieved: 6/4/16.

Smith, M. K. (2001, 2010). 'David A. Kolb on experiential learning', *the encyclopedia of informal education.* [http:// infed.org/mobi/david-a-kolb-on-experiential-learning/. Retrieved: 11 April 2016]

Stern, D. (2004).*The Present Moment in Psychotherapy and Everyday Life.* New York: Norton.

Stevens, C. (2004). Playing in the sand. *The British Gestalt Journal*, 13, 1, 18-23

Stoltenberg, C. D. and Delworth, U. (1987). *Supervising counselors and therapists.* San Francisco: Jossey-Bass.

Tennant, M. (1997). *Psychology and Adult Learning* 2e, London: Routledge.

Western, S. (2012).*Coaching and Mentoring a critical text.* London: SAGE publications.

Zuber-Skerritt, O. (1992). *Action research in higher education: examples and reflections.* London: Kogan Page.

International Coaching Federation website accessed on 5/1/15 http://coachfederation.org/credential/landing.cfm?ItemNumber=2212&navItem Number=3364&_ga=1.59116013.190452268. 1395151694&RDtoken=17852&userID=

http://www.cipd.co.uk/cpd/reflective-learning.aspx [online] accessed on 21 March 2016

http://psychology.wikia.com/wiki/Reflective_practitioner [online] accessed on 17 March 2016

http://psychologydictionary.org/self-reflection/ [online] accessed on 17 March 2016

www.oxforddictionaries.com/definition/english/self-reflection [online] accessed on 17 March 2016